N0883624

AMERICA
AFTER
NIXON

Other books by Robert Scheer
How the U.S. Got Involved in Vietnam
Diaries of Che Guevara, *editor*
Eldridge Cleaver: Post-Prison Writings and
Speeches, *editor*

with Maurice Zeitlin
Cuba: Tragedy in Our Hemisphere

AMERICA AFTER NIXON

The Age of the Multinationals

BY ROBERT SCHEER

McGraw-Hill Book Company

New York   St. Louis   San Francisco   Düsseldorf
Mexico   Panama   Toronto

JAN 17 '75

E
855
S34

Book design by Marcy J. Katz.

Copyright © 1974 by Robert Scheer.
All rights reserved. Printed in the United States of
America. No part of this publication may be reproduced,
stored in a retrieval system, or transmitted, in any form
or by any means, electronic, mechanical, photocopying,
recording, or otherwise, without the prior permission of
the publisher.

1234567890BPBP7987654

Library of Congress Cataloging in Publication Data

Scheer, Robert.
    America after Nixon.

    Includes bibliographical references.
      1. United States—Foreign relations—1969-
    2. United States—Foreign economic relations.
    3. International business enterprises. I. Title.
    E855.S34   327.73   74-13209
    ISBN 0-07-055198-7

Grateful acknowledgment is made to the following for permission to reprint material copyrighted or controlled by them:

Excerpts quoted by permission from *Foreign Affairs*, April 1972, April 1973. Copyright © 1972, 1973 by Council on Foreign Relations, Inc.

Excerpts reprinted from *The Population Bomb*, by Paul R. Ehrlich reprinted by permission of Ballantine Books, a Division of Random House, Inc. Copyright © 1968 by Paul R. Ehrlich.

Excerpts reprinted from *Economic Concentration: Structure, Behavior and Public Policy*, by J. M. Blair, with a Foreword by Gardiner C. Means, by permission of Harcourt Brace Jovanovich, Inc. Copyright © 1972 by Harcourt Brace Jovanovich, Inc.

Excerpts reprinted from *One Hundred Countries, Two Billion People*, by Robert S. McNamara by permission of the World Bank. Copyright © 1973 by Praeger Publishers, Inc.

Excerpts reprinted from *American Foreign Policy, Three Essays*, by Henry A. Kissinger by permission of W. W. Norton & Company, Inc. Copyright © 1969 by Henry A. Kissinger.

Excerpts reprinted by permission from *Time*, The Weekly Newsmagazine; Copyright Time Inc.

Excerpts reprinted from *The Oriental Economist*, July 1973, p. 16, by permission.

Excerpts reprinted from *Fortune Magazine* by permission; © 1972, 1973, Time Inc.

Excerpts reprinted from the *San Francisco Chronicle* by permission. © 1974, Chronicle Publishing Co.

Excerpts reprinted from the *Wall Street Journal* by permission. © Dow Jones & Company, Inc., 1973.

Excerpts reprinted from the *Los Angeles Times* by permission. Copyright ©, 1973, Los Angeles Times.

Excerpts reprinted from *The New York Times* by permission. © 1973, 1974 by The New York Times Company.

Excerpts reprinted from *The Washington Post* by permission. © 1970, 1974 by The Washington Post.

Excerpts reprinted from *Far Eastern Economic Review*. © 1973, 1974
Far Eastern Economic Review. Reproduced by permission.

Excerpts reprinted with permission from the December 10, 1973
and November 21, 1973 issues of *Advertising Age*. Copyright © 1973
by Crain Communications, Inc.

To Ida Kuran Scheer
and Frederick Jacob Scheer

This book owes much of its perspective to many nights of discussion with my parents after they came home from work. Despite the IRT subway and the noisy lofts of the garment district, they never became cynical or despaired of the capacity of ordinary people to make things better.

CONTENTS

Preface   Whose America? Whose World?   xi

One   America: Beyond the Cold War
    1   The Nixon Legacy   3
    2   The Vital Interests of Henry
       Kissinger   17
    3   Rockefeller's Corporate Diplomacy   37
    4   The Limits of Liberalism   63

Two   U.S. Corporations in the World
    Economy
    5   Citizens of the World   85
    6   The Growth Mania   103
    7   The Making of an Energy Crisis   127
    8   Myth of a Shrinking World   161

Three   Visions of Freedom and Waste
    9   Foreign Aid: End of an Illusion   179
    10   Asian Dollar a Day   197
    11   South Korea: The Great White
       Hope   213
    12   Ecology in China   235

Four Beyond Nixon: The Waste
        Economies and the Crisis
        of Control
    13 Dubious Détente   261
    14 America After Nixon   283

Notes   301

Acknowledgments   321

PREFACE

Whose America? Whose World?

The title *America After Nixon* does not represent simply a sigh of relief at his departure from office nor an examination of the personality of Gerald Ford. It is based rather on the notion that Nixon's troubles are symptomatic of a more general crumbling of the American political system. This age of the multinationals represents a time when effective control over what is important has passed to the new breed of transnational corporations. The ascension of Nelson Rockefeller to the Vice-Presidency merely symbolizes a process that had already been well under way. It is a process that found its ideological expression through a decade of Rockefeller Foundation and Council on Foreign Relations studies and was first implemented in what has come to be known as the Kissinger-Nixon Doctrine—a doctrine which through appeals to our obvious public desire for peace and détente leads eventually to our disenfranchisement.

It is the essential thesis of this book that the public political process no longer rules this nation, that current political debate does not deal with what is most important, and that the basic decisions about our future are being made for us by several hundred super-large multinational corporations, themselves out of control.

Neither is there any longer a strictly domestic or American life in the sense that resources, labor, cultural norms, merchandising, and even radical dissent are all now multinational in character. The corporations, through a whole new mode of operations, are the only ones who have learned to survive and take power in this new world, while the rest of us play out our tired political rituals. The breakdown of Richard Nixon revealed not only the political grease of the corporations, but also a power vacuum in which government regulatory agents, foreign diplomats, and the IRS function more as appointment secretaries for the corporations than as sources of public control.

The separation of a domestic from a foreign policy is the first act in the disenfranchisement of the American public. In the case of the energy companies (merely the most publicized case), oil executives quietly conducted the foreign policy concerned with Mideast oil resources while we were left with the more emotional questions of the Arab-Israeli dispute. The American economy is now so hopelessly intertwined with the world economy and so fully under the domination of its largest multinational corporations that any attempt to discuss our outstanding problems (be they inflation, waste, unemployment, or cultural alienation), without primary reference to the role of these corporations, is an act of deception.

During the writing of this book I was continually goaded emotionally by that spate of oil company ads with their incessant talk of "we" Americans and "our" energy problem. That they and I form a "we" has been a cherished myth of American society in the Cold War years, but one which has recently been rudely shattered, along with related ones about the efficiency and indispensability of corporate decision-making for our well-being. In 1973, John K. Jamieson, the chief executive of Exxon and owner of almost three million dollars worth of its stock, received $621,000 in total remuneration from that company.[1] The energy crisis did not affect him the same way it did us. Really it didn't. The guy responsible for those ever-earnest Mobil ads (which "we" pay for) got $500,000 for his entrepreneurial skills,[2] and probably the only people in America who think he deserved it were some executives from other large corporations and a few professional economists—a wedding of winners and losers. But this book appears at a time when it is no longer necessary to scream so loudly about the existence of class differences and the concentration of power. Such observations will become commonplace in the next period and attention will return to the serious questions of what is the majority interest, how can it come to be represented in real economic life as well as in the political theater, and what is in the interests of the world's people rather than some parochial conception of "The American Interest."

Indeed, after the rest of this book had been sent to the typesetter a Harris Poll was released which indicates that some of my most controversial propositions are increasingly obvious to people. Three out of four Americans, according to that poll, believe that the tax laws are written to help the rich and not the average man; 78 percent believe that special interests get more from the government than the people do; and 79 percent (almost four out of five Americans) now believe that the rich get richer and the poor get poorer. What these figures mean, when added to similar results in other major polls, is that the postwar dream of Corporate America as an increasingly egalitarian and democratic society is over. Or, quoting the Harris survey:

> Disenchantment with the state of the country has now reached such massive proportions among the American people that a record high 59 per cent now feel disaffected, up from 55 per cent in 1973 and more than double the 29 per cent who felt that way back in 1966.
>
> So pervasive is the feeling that no less than a majority of every single major segment of the population is turned off by politics, the [un]fairness of the economic system and the role accorded the individual in society.[3]

But to be turned off by the unfairness of the system is not equivalent to understanding why the system works that way or, better yet, what can be done about it. What we are witnessing is the emergence of a radicalism or populism that is apolitical and cynical.

This mood was to be expected, for the disclosures of government and corporate manipulation of the past ten years come on the heels of twenty-five preceding years of mindless patriotism and Cold War fanaticism. In the process we were robbed of any clear knowledge of the forces that make a society what it is. Inflation, racism, bugging, war, or high oil prices all seem part of a mosaic of injustices. Nor do these little outrages seem to have any connection to one another—they appear to be as fragmented as they are inexplicable. Our minds bounce frenetically from one to the other and soon tire of the whole piece.

Statistically recorded alienation is only in part a reason for optimism. Contrasted with the stifling uniformity of error and self-righteousness that characterized the Cold War it is of course a refreshing change. But if this mood fails to give rise to a new clarity about our system and a program for change, it will only spawn a new round of impotent rage at some "enemy" somewhere.

Part of our sense of alienation derives from the fact that during the Cold War years we were sold on the myth of America as the classless society—that we are all in the same boat. It is a good test of the degree to which we have internalized this notion that it is not

considered immediately ludicrous that John D. Rockefeller III has come to be a prophet of the need for
"revolution." He has proposed a "Second Revolution" in a book by that name that would be a laugh-
ingstock in any other advanced industrial country—
a heavy-handed Brechtian spoof.

The Rockefeller revolution is in the spirit of the
clothing, hair, and youth revolutions—the promise
of profound changes in one's life without interfering
with the existing economic relationships which are the
cutting edge. Ideas of a power elite or centers of
control are rejected out of hand as old-fashioned and
unrelated to the problems faced by the modern world.
Overpopulation becomes the safe issue.

Well, if it doesn't really matter who "owns" the
banks, then I want one, and for that I will forgo having
more than two children. But in reality, John D. Rockefeller III gets to have four kids and a bank and I get to
have guilt. Is it any wonder that most of us are alienated from the efforts of government commissions, (like
the Rockefeller one to plan for conserving our future),
when we know instinctively that the corporations
they represent will go on doing just what they want
to. To deny that the game is rigged means to capitu-
late to it; but to fail to develop a serious social alternative is to accept the stance of an isolated malcontent. We seem to have a much greater capacity to
produce Walter Mitty–type Robin Hoods and Magic
Christians than serious radicals or reformers.

The sense of political alienation carries over to the
very individuals and groups which provided the vital

impetus for change in the sixties. Although surveys now show that college students are more opposed to corporate and governmental power than at any time in the rebellious sixties, at the same time the campuses have gone over to quietism. The black population has suffered immensely from Nixon's economic policies, but the black activist movement has largely been coopted by government programs or exists primarily in prisons. The collapse of the peace movement has occurred at a time when the world, led by the U.S., is spending more on the implements of war and proportionately less on the solution to problems of poverty than ever before. And many environmentalists seem ever more concerned with marginal spills and waste and less with dismantling corporate power. Much of this is due to the fact that with the onset of the Nixon Doctrine we entered a new era of world politics and the analysis, rhetoric, and program of dissident groups was caught off guard.

This is a book about politics after the Cold War; about America's life as well as its role in a world that now knows very different power configurations and issues than the ones which dominated our attention these past years. In the period after World War II, it was presumed that basic economic problems had been solved, and that we had entered the age of the affluent society.

But we are now witnessing a reassertion of the economic issues of the thirties on a global level. The predictions of the futurists of a postscarcity society in which our food needs would be solved by compressed alfalfa pills and our energy needs by free nuclear power have not come to pass. The world is now dominated by a great preoccupation with growth and scarcity, and the extreme contradictions between the rich and the poor in the world economy are now more intense than in Marx's bleakest predictions.

That there is a majority world interest that is being betrayed is the primary preoccupation of this book. People don't write books of this sort simply because of reading a Harris Poll or stumbling upon some interesting data in the library. My perceptions are not disinterested and they did not arise spontaneously after signing this book contract. For the past fifteen years I have "covered" stories in many of the world's ghettos—that Third World outside the main economies which includes sections of Oakland as well as Southeast Asia. During that time I came to understand that the visible signs of the modern culture—Chase, Exxon, Marlboro, Motorola, GM—which I saw everywhere, were also the new symbols of power. That was obvious but what confused me was why this overwhelming business activity hardly ever appeared in political news reporting. The best explanation that I could come up with was that we reporter-types had come to accept (or celebrate in some cases) the international-corporate-consumer culture as a given of modern life. One does not have to report on a given—it is like describing oxygen—for better or worse, it exists, and we have grown dependent upon it.

Had I not also traveled to North Vietnam, North

Korea, Cuba, and China, the consumerist fix might have held longer. But visiting China in the fall of 1970, just after the Cultural Revolution, I encountered a society in which 800 million human beings managed to survive somehow without deodorants, an elaborate pet industry, Sears garbage compactors, or even the private auto. Whether that was good or bad, was to me less pressing than that modern corporate capitalism was not an inevitable given of economic development—that there are other models and that in the post–Cold War era one will at last have the occasion to publicly investigate them. It is also a model which will have increasing appeal to the poorer countries who have attempted to follow the U.S.-exported "free-world model" and who, despite our government's insistence on its virtues, find themselves further behind us than they were when they started. To these people the Chinese argument that the basic contradiction in the world is between the poor and the rich must contain a certain compelling logic. It is an argument which we are now forced to take more seriously even within our own society and for that reason it forms a central theme of this book.

I dedicated this book to my mother, not only for the obvious reasons, but also because what I learned from her experiences gave me some insight into why two out of three Americans now tell the Gallup Poll that inflation is their most pressing problem. After forty-six years of full-time work in sweater factories and faithfully paying her taxes and union dues, she is now expected to live on $267 a month. That's $192 from Social Security, and $75 from the International Ladies Garment Workers Union, which has been much-publicized as a progressive union. Millions of retired people survive on much less; others do a little better. It was important for me to understand that although I get to write books or Henry Kissinger gets to be Secretary of State, these are not in themselves victories for economic democracy or proof of general social mobility.

I was taught at Christopher Columbus High School in the Bronx that we no longer have classes in America. But to confess my bias, nothing I've seen or read since has disproved my schoolyard perception that most people get screwed and a few do the screwing.

What comes later in this book is not in any sense neutral and hopefully not dispassionate. I want to know what's going on and for that reason I follow the evidence carefully, but I also know that the system as it works is not great. The other day somebody in an Irish Republican bar in Oakland leaned over to me and in a drunken whisper said, "Eat the rich—pass it on." I wasn't yet drunk, and first and properly thought that to be a rather immature and nonprogrammatic suggestion. But what the hell—it's a lot more to the point than Beat Stanford or Kill Gooks and if it catches on at least there will be something more to talk about. (I have left a note that my editor should leave in this last because the tendency would be to cut something so flippant out of a "nonfiction" book, with its inevitable above-it-all air. But I didn't write this book from the above-it-all.) So let me make one thing perfectly clear. I never liked Nixon because he tried to get away with what we couldn't and was self-righteous about it. But the Rockefellers and the Kennedys didn't even need such petty gambits. I can sympathize with the hustles of Nixon because he still felt the necessity to put a little something aside for his family—a job for his brother, a few jewels for Pat, a nice house they could be proud of after. The fact that he was "worried about his future" is understandable to me. But it is also a pathetic display of social ineptness, not to mention false consciousness; he should've known they would never let him get away with it. He was moving too fast and too low instead of biding his time waiting for the more respectable goodies that were yet to come—a million-dollar biography, the presidency of a top college, or running the Ford Foundation. Richard Nixon's training has proven inadequate to the great task of laying up a little while running this nation, and he has made it that much harder for a lower-middle-class kid to rise to his country's heights. But for all of my excitement at seeing this grubnik turned out, I will not for a minute accept the idea that his crimes were the only important ones or that his departure guarantees our freedom. Just looking at him you knew that this guy was not the boss.

The following chapters do not uncover a conspiracy theory or the "boss" behind it all. The modern world political economy is a complicated thing, as is America's role in it. Power is often exercised in subtle and even contradictory ways. Nixon's political adventures, although ominous enough, were only a small part of what has come to be the American way of life. He operated in a rapidly shifting environment, and we should not take his personal overreaching as a denial of his serious commitment to the objectives of corporate America. It is these more basic interests and questions of power that form the substance of this book's inquiry.

part one

AMERICA: BEYOND THE COLD WAR

chapter 1

THE NIXON LEGACY

Richard Nixon presided over the dissolution of the Cold War and with it of an artificial unity that had persisted for a quarter of a century, distorting the public's perceptions of power and rule. He was to be numbered among the first casualties of the thaw. It is ironic that he who did so much in the fifties to rally us against the external devils had been left by a twist of history to face us sputtering and alone—a cheerleader without a game.

Nixon had been forced by events beyond his control to disarm himself and the politics he espoused. This was evidenced by the actions of the Nixon team which came to be characterized by a thrashing about with one set of policies undermining the logic of another. At the same moment that the President and Kissinger were secretly working out a détente with the Chinese and Russian communists, the President, in a fit of paranoia about domestic subversion, hired old anticommunist spooks and Cuban refugees to spy on his own staff. Despite Kissinger's claim in September of 1973 that this was "the first time since the war that we have had a world that is at peace,"[1] a month later the President asked for the biggest defense budget in the history of the nation.

The concern for "national security" was Nixon's main prop in the Watergate follies. And he defended the burglary of Daniel Ellsberg's psychiatrist's office on the grounds that Ellsberg might have been dealing with enemy agents. But such arguments no longer worked. What was the percentage in accusing Ellsberg of talking to a Russian when Nixon himself had drunk Mai Tai with Chou En-lai? Nixon's foreign policy had destroyed the rationale for his domestic one.

The death of anticommunism as the binding force of American rule here and abroad opened a Pandora's box. When the Arab oil producers became uppity, we could no longer quietly land the Special Forces Advisers to save freedom. Domestically, the implications have been even more startling. A politically desensitized America, numbed by a quarter century of anticommunism, has started to ask very provocative questions about who runs America and for whom. In this new context Watergate has become a radical poli-sci course. Its most shattering implication being that the mythical "we" of the civics classes do not decide things—that there is, in fact, a "they" of corporations, lobbyists, and bureaucrats who determine almost everything from the price of milk to the mergers of multinational corporations.

For twenty-five years of Cold War, most social scientists had stuck doggedly to an incredibly naive view of the American political process—a vision of roughly equal pluralistic grouplets contending and compromising for power. Then Shazaam! the clothes come off and some of these groups turn out to be mere subsidiaries of the conglomerates who finance the events of democracy, while most of us have simply been disenfranchised. The Presidency has turned out to be a brokerage house for corporate favors which treats the citizenry as a basically irrelevant "constant" (not even an interesting variable) in the computer's cal-

P9 285

culations. But in the wake of Watergate that public has now begun to set off little explosions. Consequently, the most important result of the end of the Cold War may turn out to be the revival of American democracy and with it the beginning of serious debate about the role of the large corporations in the formulation of public policy.

The best clue as to why the Cold War ended is not to be found in some stolen document or obscure tome, but rather in the most public pronouncements of the 37th President himself, that collection of annual speeches to the Congress on the state of the world which formed the Nixon Doctrine. It represents the first major break in postwar strategy and its impact will be felt long after Nixon's departure from the Presidency.

The Truman Doctrine signaled the onset of that era of containment and confrontation known as the Cold War, and the Nixon Doctrine represented a major shift to a very new era of relations between the capitalist and communist giants. But whereas the Truman Doctrine developed because of the needs of an expanding American empire, the Nixon Doctrine was a response to the needs of an empire that was disintegrating.

Since Nixon personally loved and politically needed the Cold War as much as any American, we must ask why he officiated at its death. For the answer we must take a hard look at the changes registered in the world's political and economic life between 1954, when Nixon was in favor of dropping nuclear weapons on North Vietnam to stop the spread of Chinese communism, and 1973, when he signed a peace agreement with North Vietnam partially to further "our friendship with China."

Richard Nixon has always been underestimated by his detractors, who have tended to view him as a red-baiting fanatic or simply as a prisoner of petty ambition. It is more accurate to see him as a conduit of elite political signals. He has always been less the obsessed anticommunist ideologue and more perfectly the amoral corporate lawyer. To fail to understand this is to deny his flexibility or the capacity for opportunism which was his real genius. An obsessed man could not have delivered the Nixon Doctrine, for it is devoid of any core commitment and is, rather, a memo to a client about cutting losses and bringing the company out of a downward spiral. It has all the moral fervor of Laurence Harvey playing Chairman of the Board.

The Nixon Doctrine begins with the pragmatic assertion that the system is not working: "This administration must lead the nation through a fundamental transition in foreign policy . . . we are at the end of an era. The postwar order of international relations—the configuration of power that emerged from the Second World War is gone. With it are gone the conditions which have determined the assumptions and practice of United States foreign policy since 1945."[2]

What is gone is an era of expanding American power. It would not be oversimplistic to view the quarter of a century following the Second World War as one in which the overriding dynamic was the attempt by the U.S. to establish hegemony over world politics. The United States emerged from the Second World War with the only (modern) economy that was not only intact but actually stronger than it had been before the war. The economies of Western Europe, Russia, and of course, Germany and Japan were in shambles. The U.S. alone was in the position to make loans, provide ships, and threaten the peace of those who didn't go along. It also possessed a nuclear monopoly.

Of course, the U.S. rationale for the Cold War was built on quite the opposite assertion—that a strong and aggressive Soviet Union had a plan for the international takeover of the "free world," and that unless the U.S. moved to contain that force, the Soviet timetable would be realized.

Whatever one may think of the quality of political life in the Soviet Union of that period, it should no longer be necessary to argue this point. Not only do we now possess abundant historical records in the form of memoirs and the minutes of various international conferences, we also know that the U.S. officials who spread this nonsense knew full well that the opposite was true.

It used to be argued by those who served the Truman government that the Soviet Union broke the "friendly mood" of the wartime alliance by gobbling up Eastern Europe and unleashing guerrilla warfare and subversion throughout Asia, and that only the timely response of Truman's Cold War containment stopped it. That was a pretty effective argument before most of us had a chance to read the minutes of the Yalta, Tehran, and Potsdam conferences. Now that the minutes have been released, we know not only the details of the type of caviar and wine that was served, but also how blocks of territories were divided. In the crudest terms, the Soviet Union was "given" Eastern Europe, the U.S. and its allies "took" the rest of the world.[3]

The Soviets had been badly hurt in the war with forty million casualties and all major cities leveled. Panicked by the revival of a German militarism propped up once again by the Western capitalists, and, still thinking in old-fashioned military terms of land invasion, they wanted a buffer zone on their eastern flank. This was slightly ridiculous in a developing age of nuclear weapons and B-52s. (But, then again, no one ever accused Stalin of being an advanced thinker.) In return for this buffer, the Soviets gave up the struggle in those places where they had real strength. The French and Italian Communist Parties were told to lay dawn their arms and participate in rigged elections. The Vietnamese and other colonized people were told to wait for their emancipation until the Communists of France and England were voted into power and could then free them. The Greek and Philippine guerrilla movements were simply abandoned to the mercies of the English and American occupation forces. And the Communist Chinese were issued a go-slow order. As to the American

Communists, they were even instructed at one point (or at least such was the interpretation of then Chairman Browder), to go out of business and join the Democratic Party.[4]

So what was the threat of this communism to the free world, and who perceived it? Certainly not Winston Churchill who was present when Roosevelt gave Poland to Stalin and Greece to England. Not Kennan or Harriman who took minutes of the meetings, nor Truman who received all such documents on assuming office. Yet it was this same Winston Churchill who made the famous Fulton, Mo., speech attacking Russian treachery in entering Eastern Europe—a speech most often credited with launching the Western position in the Cold War.* Truman, who was on the stage, offered full agreement. What was in their minds?

The world had come out of the war with what some called a revolution of rising expectations. Anticolonialism was the order of the day, and ordinary people in both the developed and poor countries shared a general antipathy toward the reassertion of empire. The free-world imagery provided necessary cover behind which the U.S. government attempted to orchestrate a new order of power relations. Bolshevism had been

---

* For all the publicity that followed the publication of the second installment of Khrushchev's memoirs, no one noticed that Khrushchev denied the stock arguments for the U.S. position in the Cold War. In reference to Churchill's Fulton attack, Khrushchev said, "It was largely because of Churchill's speech that Stalin exaggerated our enemies' strength and their intention to unleash war on us. As a result he became obsessed with shoring up our defenses against the West."[5]

a real scare since its inception, but as an idea and program, rather than a threat from a Soviet army. The desire to destroy Bolshevism before it spread had been basic to American policy since the landing of U.S. troops on Archangel in 1919. It had led to the Anglo-U.S. coddling of Hitler in the hopes he would turn East, and to American hesitancy to enter the war and then open a second front. But Bolshevism was feared as revolution, indigenous and popular, not as Soviet expansionism. The post–World War II plan was to contain the fire of revolution among the "have-nots," reassert the power of the "haves," and defeat socialism in the industrialized countries of Europe. In short, the establishment of the hegemony of Western capitalism.

This could best be accomplished by identifying the cause of empire with the cause of self-determination and freedom. Hence the creation of a devil—international communism.

The first sticky part in all this came with the efforts of the French and English "partners of democracy" to rebuild their old-fashioned empires. But the first Indochina war and the continuing "troubles" in Algeria finished off that idea. The U.S. finally abandoned support of such traditional colonial ventures, and instead insisted on a neo-colonialist model with native "democratic" leaders—a Ngo Dinh Diem replacing a Bao Dai. This system worked until the Cuban revolution and the second Indochina war. The emergence of successful, indigenous popular revolutionary forces in the sixties tore away the mask of America's Cold War posture, forced increasing reliance on the use of American troops, and ended with the alienation of the world's people (including Americans) from the "goals" of U.S. foreign policy. The effort to assert American hegemony became untenable—it was being defeated militarily, it was too costly both in dollars and resources, it ran up against growing contradictions between the U.S. and increasingly powerful Western European and Japanese rivals, and it was incapable of responding to the incredible changes occurring within the communist world.

In popular language, all this came to be talked about in the vocabulary of overextension—"we can't be the world's cop," "we can't be everywhere," "wrong war at the wrong time," etc. As Nixon stated:

> In the era of American predominance, we resorted to American prescriptions as well as resources. In the new era, our friends are revitalized and increasingly self-reliant, while the American domestic consensus has been strained by 25 years of global responsibilities.[6]

And in the very next paragraph he gives the lie to the whole earlier free-world defense posture by saying:

> In the era of overwhelming U.S. military strengths, we and our allies could rely on the doctrine of massive retaliation. In the new era, growing Soviet power has altered the military equation. Failure to adapt to this change could lead to confrontations which pose an agonizing choice between paralysis and holocaust. Strength that served the cause of peace during a

period of relative superiority needs new definitions
to keep the peace during a period of relative equality.[7]

What, then, are the configurations of such peace?
Why did détente come when the Soviet army was
strong and not when it was weak? If the Russians
were the aggressors in the Cold War because of the
nature of their system, then one would have thought
it easier to negotiate when they were weak. Nixon's
argument could only make sense if we were the
aggressors, for then their increased strength could
force us into negotiation and détente. Is this not also
true of China? The words "peace" and "U.S. hegemony" were used synonymously in the Cold War, the
former as an acceptable cover for the latter. And now
that we must settle for something less than hegemony,
that too will be synonymous with peace. It is not
that communism has changed but rather that our
sights have been set toward less ambitious goals.

If U.S. power had been able to win decisively in
Vietnam, then things would have been different, at
least temporarily. But it was already clear from the
failure of the Johnson policy that the U.S. war was a
loser. What a half million American troops and
"moderate" bombing could not do, Nixon attempted
with massive bombing, blockades, and expanding the
war to Cambodia. But it was really just the old college try—rear-guard action to assure he would not be
charged with appeasement when he moved to cut
losses through a negotiated peace.

Although that peace had been offered in substantially the same form by the Vietnamese revolutionaries some eight years before, it was nonetheless pictured as victory, not because of any specific commitments in Vietnam, but rather so that more essential parts of America's foreign policy could be salvaged. The people must not confuse the "quagmire" of Vietnam with our "necessary presence" in the Middle East or Latin America. As Nixon put it:

> The American people have grown somewhat weary of 25 years of international burdens. This weariness was coming in any event, but the anguish of the Vietnam war hastened it, or at least our awareness of it. Many Americans, frustrated by the conflict in Southeast Asia, have been tempted to draw the wrong conclusions . . . there is also a lesson not to be drawn: that the only antidote for undifferentiated involvement is indiscriminate retreat.

> Our experience in the 1960s has underlined the fact that we should not do more abroad than domestic opinion can sustain. But we cannot let the pendulum swing in the other direction, sweeping us towards an isolationism which could be as disastrous as excessive zeal. . . . The Nixon doctrine will enable us to remain committed in ways that we can sustain.[8]

The new course of our foreign policy is avowedly globalist in that it occurs at a time when America is more dependent than ever on the outside world for resources and markets. In the face of heightened competition and tension it does not abandon the goal of control, but rather aims at what Nixon called "a new, more subtle form of leadership." ". . . We do not rule out new commitments, but we will relate them to our interests. . . . Our objective, in the first instance, is to support our *interests* [his italics] over the long run with a sound foreign policy. . . . Our interests must shape our commitments"[9]

What then are these interests which Nixon chose to italicize?

chapter 2

THE VITAL
INTERESTS
OF
HENRY KISSINGER

When Richard Nixon offered Henry Kissinger the post of National Security Adviser in his incoming administration, there was a sense of surprised relief throughout what has been known as the Eastern foreign-policy establishment. Henry Kissinger had been one of their prize protégés. He had run the CIA-funded Harvard International Center, and later was Associate Director of its prestigious Center for International Affairs. In the fifties, he had emerged as a prime example of what C. Wright Mills termed the Crackpot Realists, a hardheaded student of the various options of nuclear weaponry and policy, and a firm believer in balance-of-power tactics. Before joining Nixon, he had worked for over a dozen years as a sort of secretary of state to the Rockefeller Foundation, assisting in its many reports about the goals and tactics of U.S. foreign policy. He was also a frequent contributor to proceedings of the Council on Foreign Relations and its magazine *Foreign Affairs.* The composition of this last group, without debating specifics, is certainly as close as America comes to having a ruling class prerogative in foreign-policy matters. (Three out of the last five Secretaries of State have worked for the Rockefeller Foundation and all were associated with the Council on Foreign Relations.)

Heinz Alfred Kissinger represented the opposite extreme to the bulk of Nixon's other appointees. He was not a trusted political crony. He and Nixon had met only once at a Clare Boothe Luce cocktail party, and Henry would have thought it vulgar to have worked in any of Richard's campaigns, let alone get into real estate deals with him. Nixon's palace guard, the veterans of Southern California politics, regarded Henry as a suspect intellectual immigrant, who for all the intense anticommunism of his writings, was probably a secret pinko. They were never to get along.

But Nixon chose Kissinger and, in this uncharacteristic appointment, revealed that however much he may have possessed the insecurities and attendant failings of mainsteam America, he was willing to take his cues from the Eastern establishment in matters of foreign policy.

That establishment, throughout the last years of the sixties, had been developing a view that American foreign policy was an unworkable treadmill. America was overextended, supermoral, a prisoner of humanitarian fantasies, and unaware of its declining power relative to the rest of the world. To continue on the course of empire building would be counterproductive to what had been gained in terms of economic power and prestige. The war in Vietnam had been instrumental in forcing such a reexamination, but there were other factors: the rise of Soviet military power, the growing independence and stability of Communist China, Japanese economic development and Western European unity. A policy based on overwhelming American strength had grown unwieldy, had alienated important sections of the American public as well as those abroad, and lacked the flexibility to act decisively where interests required it. Kennedy had been frenetic and Johnson obsessed, and neither posture was judged very useful by the men of the boardrooms.

Kissinger caught that mood quite early and wrote extensively about alternatives during the same period that Richard Nixon, with his very sensitive political nose, sniffed that both the average person and the rich and powerful were increasingly uneasy with America's world role.

The Council on Foreign Relations had commissioned a far-reaching analysis of the weaknesses and future options for American foreign policy in two major sets of book-length studies, one on China policy and the other on Europe/U.S. relations called the *Atlantic Policy Studies.* Kissinger, who had been the Council's Director of Nuclear Weapons and Foreign Policy Studies, authored one book in the series, *The Troubled Partnership,* and assisted on others. These studies provided the basis for the overhauling of American foreign policy which came to be known as the Nixon Doctrine.

The China studies essentially argued that communism was there to stay, and that any notion of unleashing Chiang Kai-shek to retake the mainland was hopeless nonsense. The studies made quite clear that students of these matters, including those in government, did not take seriously the then official government line that Chinese communist aggression was the source of revolution or instability in the world. Indeed, at the very time when the American public was still being told we had to stop the

communists in Vietnam because they were directed
by the ChiComs, these studies refuted that notion
by asserting the obvious reality of multipolarity
in the communist world, and established that certainly Vietnam and North Korea were independent
of China and Russia.

Since it would be pointless to attempt to overthrow
Communist China, the pro-Chiang policy gave way to
other options such as negotiation with Mao and the
possibilities of exacerbating the Sino-Soviet split. The
Council on Foreign Relations even commissioned a
public opinion survey from the Survey Research
Center at Michigan University which showed that the
American public would approve of an American President negotiating with China *and even visiting that
country.* That survey was taken in 1964, and it took six
more years of bombing Indochina in the name of stopping the commies before an American President
would give up the ghost of that Cold War posture and
"dare" to normalize relations with China—something
the American people had been willing to accept all
along.

A similar realism characterized the view of European policy. Ostensibly based on the notion of defending Western Europe against Soviet attacks, this
policy in reality had far more to do with U.S. economic
penetration of those countries and increasing European resistance.

One of the more insightful contributions of Kissinger's study was his observation that the problems
we were experiencing with De Gaulle were not a

result of the man's haughtiness but rather of changing power relations.

> No one man could have disrupted the Alliance by himself. Fundamental changes have been taking place in the relative weights of Europe and the United States, in the nature of alliances and in the character of strategy. Allied relationships would have had to be adapted to new conditions, no matter who governed in Paris—or in Washington, for that matter.[1]

As in the other studies in this series, Kissinger's analysis was based on an awareness that the era of American predominance had passed and that we had to adapt to that change:

> Perhaps the deepest danger we face is that, as with all great achievements, nostalgia for the patterns of action that were appropriate when America was predominant and Europe impotent may become an obstacle to the creativity needed to deal with an entirely new situation.[2]

Kissinger published this work in 1965 when it was too early to foretell the full impact of the defeat of American strategy in Vietnam, but it was clear that the age of hegemony was over, and it is instructive to examine the reasons he offered then for its end:

> The period of American hegemony came to an end in the late fifties and early sixties under the impact of four events in which United States policy had played a major role: European economic recovery; European integration; decolonization; and the Cuban missile crisis and its aftermath. Each of these events illus-

trates that results cannot always be judged by the intentions of those whose policies start an historical process, even less by their pronouncements.[3]

These changes are reflected not only in Europe's bilateral relations with the U.S. on matters of tariffs and multinational corporate investment, but also in the European attitude toward the Third World and the communist countries. When Kissinger wrote of the impact of decolonization, it was Europe's decolonization that he was referring to and not that of the United States. Europe's loss of her colonies had put her in an objectively different position than the U.S. vis-à-vis the Third World. As Kissinger stated, "We are now the only member of NATO with world-wide interests, and this produces unavoidable differences in perspective."[4]

Not possessing these farflung interests, European nations were unwilling to support the U.S. in Vietnam in any serious way: "If our allies give assistance, it will be token in nature, and the motive will be to obtain a veto over United States actions. The thrust of their recommendations will be to avoid a direct showdown and even the semblance of risk."[5]

The prophetic accuracy of that statement was evidenced nine years later when, as Secretary of State, Kissinger failed in his attempt to line up the European governments in a collective bloc against the Arabs and Persians on the oil price question. In fact, they went it alone and made their own deals, and not necessarily the ones the American oil companies would have wanted. Here, as elsewhere in the Third

World, the U.S. had displaced the older colonialists. And as Kissinger had predicted; "Our European Allies have a psychological block against running major risks on behalf of areas from which they have been so recently ejected."[6]

Not only do the U.S. and Europe have differences in regard to the Third World, but also in negotiating with the major communist powers, particularly the Soviet Union. The Soviet-U.S. détente alarmed the West Europeans in much the same way it did the Chinese communists—as a new effort to divide up the world.

The "threat" of communism had been used globally by the U.S. to keep other countries in line, the way it was used domestically to stifle opposition to government policies. So when the U.S. chose to have a détente with the Soviets, they lost that weapon for instilling obedience. "As the Soviet threat appears to recede, the scope for largely national action widens proportionately."[7]

Kissinger's argument here is similar to the Nixon Doctrine statement. Once the glue of anticommunism is lost, it will be more difficult to develop consensus behind U.S. policies until new methods are developed:

> Defense against a military threat will soon lose its force as a political bond. Negotiations with the East will prove corrosive unless they go hand in hand with the creation of common political purposes and the institutions to embody them. The need, in short, is to go from alliances to community.[8]

At the time of that writing, Kissinger had not found the basis for such a community, nor did he as Secretary of State. For the sources of the conflict which he delineated have tended to increase rather than recede. He was correct in understanding that the old way was no longer tenable, but it is easier to *cut losses* (which he has done brilliantly) than to start new profitable ventures.

Kissinger's focus was on Europe, but similar points were made by other Council on Foreign Relations studies of the rest of the world, and all carried the same limitation. They expressed a stark awareness of the problem, but became vague as to solutions, and ended by calling wanly for flexibility and creativity. It is this ambivalence which characterizes the freshness but also the weakness of the Nixon Doctrine.

A preview of the Nixon Doctrine appeared in a collection of essays published in late 1968 by the Ford Foundation and the Brookings Institute entitled *Agenda for the Nation.* Henry Brandon, the London *Sunday Times* Washington correspondent who was once a confidant of Nixon and Kissinger, states that the Brookings book was intended "as a guide and inspiration for the incoming President."[9]

In the concluding essay, "Central Issues of American Foreign Policy," Kissinger offered the outlines and, indeed, actual phrases of what was to become much of the Nixon Doctrine. The concepts of the essay are simple, in some ways a refreshing departure from the past pretensions of American foreign policy, but in Kissinger's special style they are essentially negative and rhetorical without appearing to be either: a prescription for dealing with past mistakes without a vision of what the future will or should bring.

The essay reflects a very definite understanding that the U.S. became overextended and, for all of its military power, found its political power eroding. The Soviets were in an equivalent military position to make our worst nuclear threats too costly for either side to contemplate. And lesser weapons, as Vietnam illustrated most notably, had failed to bring acquiescence. Unable to use its nuclear strength and faced with a relative erosion of its political and economic options, the U.S. empire was running out of steam. A prisoner of unworkable strategies, it was mired down in commitments which could not produce results and seemed endless in duration. With its resources strained internationally, with competing domestic demands, growing opposition in both the developed and underdeveloped worlds, and the disaffection of American youth, it was no longer possible to go on.

Kissinger was not among those who discounted the domestic victories of the New Left and, in particular, the alienation of youth from the purposes of empire:

> Today, however, many in the younger generation consider the management of power irrelevant, perhaps even immoral. . . . The new ethic of freedom is not "civic," it is indifferent or even hostile to systems and notions of order. Management is equated with manipulation. Structural designs are perceived as systems of "domination"—not of order. The generation

which has come of age after the fifties has had Vietnam as its introduction to world politics.[10]

In the Nixon Doctrine this disaffection over Vietnam is made more explicit, and at one point, it is
stated that to attempt to win on the battlefield would
be devastating; "It would have split apart our own
society. . . . In other countries there was growing
strength and autonomy. In our own there was nas-
cent isolationism in reaction to overextension. In the
light of these changed conditions we could not continue on the old path."[11]

This was not a matter of psychological ennui but
rather the resurgence of a relatively healthy isolationism, as Americans recognized that they were not benefiting from U.S. penetration and intervention. It was
not a matter of people's indifference to questions of
world poverty or other pressing problems, but an understanding that our foreign policy was exacerbating,
rather than contributing to a solution of those problems. At no time in the Cold War period were the
American people ever given a serious choice of devot-
ing a significant commitment of resources to solving
problems of poverty, not as an addition to military
spending but as an alternative, or at least partial alternative to it. What they did reject in the sixties was the
continual outlay and waste of resources and lives without apparent benefit to anyone.

With the dramatic expansion of our troops in
Vietnam (from thirteen thousand to half a million),
the material costs of our commitment in Southeast

Asia became more apparent. Financially, it put a serious strain on America's balance of payments. Militarily, it very much restricted the possibility of U.S. intervention in other more strategically vital areas. As Kissinger stated in his earlier essay:

> Whatever the outcome of the war in Vietnam, it is clear that it has greatly diminished American willingness to become involved in this form of warfare elsewhere. Its utility as a precedent has therefore been importantly undermined.[12]

The new realism about America's options was the decisive idea of the Kissinger essay and the other studies. It would be a mistake to underestimate the degree of departure the new policy took from that which had dominated the twenty-five years before. But it is best to let Kissinger summarize it himself: "The United States is no longer in a position to operate programs globally; it has to encourage them. It can no longer impose its preferred solution; it must seek to evoke it."[13]

The Nixon Doctrine stresses that America has "interests"— not simply moral concerns—that must be pursued, an emphasis which seems hardheaded enough in Kissingerese: "It is part of American folklore that while other nations have interests, we have responsibilities. . . . A mature conception of our interest in the world would obviously have to take into account the widespread interest in stability and peaceful change."[14] But again, what is that mature interest?

When Kissinger writes: "We find it hard to articulate a truly vital interest which we would defend
however 'legal' the challenge,"[15] is he saying that *he
could* articulate such an interest, and would it cover
something like another country's legal nationalization
of an American corporation's affiliate?

He puts down old Secretary Rusk quite hand-
ily: "We have a tendency to offer our altruism as a
guarantee of our reliability; 'We have no quarrel
with the Communists,' Secretary Rusk said on one
occasion; 'all of our quarrels are on behalf of other
people.' "[16] Now Kissinger tells us he knows better—
that we have interests and they are not related to such
abstractions as a fear of enemy aggression:

> This leads to an undifferentiated globalism and con-
> fusion about our purposes. The abstract concept of
> aggression causes us to multiply our commitments.
> But the denial that our interests are involved dimin-
> ishes our staying power when we try to carry out
> these commitments.[17]

But if you give up the aggression gambit, you sac-
rifice consensus. For aggression is presumably against
all of us. The old refrain of "If we don't stop them
in Vietnam, we'll have to do it in San Diego," had a
certain national logic. If "they" are out to invade
"our" country, then we have a common stake in
resisting. But if "they" are merely demanding control
of some part of their economy in which, say, the U.S.-
owned multinational corporations have a stake, then
most of us might not think "our" interests are involved.

As ludicrous as it appears in retrospect, it once seemed plausible to suggest that Castro and his six million Cubans must be stopped lest, as part of an international communist army, they aggress against us. But if we can live with eight hundred million Chinese communists (and they are at odds with Castro anyway) then where is the threat of aggression?

The Russian and Chinese détentes have robbed American foreign policy of its appearance of representing a "classless" vision. Kissinger understands this problem and implies that the future will be much more disorderly without the old myths. His history is poor and he skips over some fairly intense class struggle in America, but he is certainly accurate about its suppression during the Cold War years;

> At least until the emergence of the race problem, we were blessed by the absence of conflicts between classes and over ultimate ends. These factors produced the characteristic aspects of American foreign policy: a certain manipulativeness and pragmatism, a conviction that the normal pattern of international relations was harmonious, a reluctance to think in structural terms, a belief in final answers—all qualities which reflect a sense of self-sufficiency not far removed from a sense of omnipotence. Yet the contemporary dilemma is that there are no total solutions; we live in a world gripped by revolutions in technology, values and institutions.[18]

While this is not exactly a full-blown Marxist understanding of the international class struggle, it does convey a sense of foreboding about the future grand design going over.

The design of the Kissinger-Nixon Doctrine was fundamentally flawed in that it moved away from one source of cohesion for American foreign policy without being able to substitute an alternative acceptable to most Americans. Based as it was on the vision of an external threat or devil, anticommunism could unite all classes and interest groups behind a broad range of policies which otherwise would be divisive. It was the basis for the elimination of radicals from the labor movement as well as from the universities. It enlisted factory workers and corporate heads, small farmers and big food chains, all in the same "moral" crusade for world freedom. During the height of the Cold War it bordered on the subversive to even challenge that unity of interest. Irrational appeals to national jingoism could be inveighed against "pinkos" in rank-and-file union caucuses or against independent minded TV commentators.

American foreign policy during the Cold War years was directed more toward maintaining domestic tranquility than in holding back a real enemy. The use of anticommunism as a domestic weapon for averting all of the class tensions of the thirties had an immense appeal to those with a stake in such stability, and accounts for their enthusiasm for a policy that must always have seemed absurd to insiders. Those interests supported Truman rather than Henry Wallace not because they thought Truman had made a *correct* assessment of the Soviet Union, but because his assessment was convenient and even necessary to the maintenance of their power.

It is naive to think that in 1969 we suddenly discovered that China was not a military threat after all,
and that the Soviet Union had to be bargained with.
After 1965–69, the years of the Cultural Revolution,
when we began to consider the possibilities of détente, China was, in fact, far more radical than it had
been in 1950, when we were most opposed to communism of any sort.

The Soviets barely had an economy, let alone
nuclear weapons in the first years of Cold War, and
by Kissinger's own reckoning, only attained nuclear
parity with us after the Cuban missile crisis of 1962,
precisely the period when we moved toward détente
with them.

The growth of communist power in all of its
varied and divided forms, from Soviet weaponry
to Vietnamese insurgency, has made the continuance
of empire very costly. But as our policy was checked,
this anticommunism became unworkable as a moral
and unifying goal for the American people as well as
our "free-world allies." Beginning with the Bay of
Pigs and continuing through the entire Vietnam War,
the pretenses of America's "containment of aggression" policy were stripped away. Anticommunism,
instead of being a unifying force, became a divisive
one within the American body politic and abroad.
And so it was dropped as abruptly as it had been
taken up twenty-five years earlier, again for reasons
quite opposite to the publicly stated ones.

Nixon stated in a definition of his Doctrine: ". . .
To continue our predominant contribution might not

have been beyond our physical resources—though our own domestic programs summoned them. But it certainly would have exceeded our psychological resources."[19]

This concept of "psychological" strain, which Kissinger also uses frequently, really translates into the American people's refusal to buy the system any more. Even Republican Senator (now Attorney General) Saxbe stated after the Nixon bombing of Hanoi that the President had "taken leave of his senses." Anticommunism had become untenable as a belief system and had therefore lost its usefulness. A new way was required:

> Thus while lowering our overseas presence and direct military involvement, our new policy calls for a new form of leadership. This policy must not only reflect a changed public will. It must shape a new consensus for a balanced and positive American role.
>
> . . . The Nixon Doctrine will enable us to remain committed in ways that we can sustain. The solidity of domestic support in turn will reverberate overseas with continued confidence in American performance.[20]

That was stated on February 25, 1971, and we all know what happened to the "solidity of domestic support" for Nixon's policies since that time. And it was not just "Watergate." As I stated earlier, if there had been a new "consensus" with the cohesive strength of the old anticommunism then Watergate would have been pushed under the rug in the interest of national security. It didn't work because there was no new consensus.

The reaction to the Cambodian invasion, held up as a prime example of Nixon's "new policy," and perhaps the most divisive action of any President in American history, should have indicated that the new consensus would not hold.

The difficulty of forming this consensus becomes even clearer when we attempt to apply it to the area of the world which Nixon indicated was critical to our "interests"—the Mideast:

> The Middle East is a place today . . . where the vital interests of the United States and the Soviet Union are both involved. . . . Vietnam is our most anguishing problem. It is not, however, the most dangerous. That grim distinction must go to the situation in the Middle East with its vastly greater potential for drawing Soviet policy and our own into a collision that could prove uncontrollable.[21]

But why is it so "dangerous"? There is not a single major government on any side within the area that is "communist." None of them have aggressive designs on U.S. territory. On what basis could "we Americans" form a consensus? Is it around historical Arab-Israeli disputes that all of us could find a common interest; or around the disposition of Mideast oil; or the relation of the American oil companies to the Arab governments; or the possibility of increased Soviet control of that oil; or the Suez Canal? What has become clear in the whole energy crisis caper is that, once shorn of the anticommunist-aggressor rationale, "we" are not so unified about our vital Middle East interests. That rubric had been very con-

venient for enlisting public support in overthrowing
governments that threatened the oil companies. But
in the recent crisis, a growing number of Americans
did not feel that they and the oil companies did, in
fact, have the same interests.

Indeed, as it transpired, the oil companies made
enormous profits while most Americans suffered
higher prices and fuel cuts; and strong evidence
indicated that the oil companies colluded with Arab
governments to cheat on their U.S. income taxes.
Would it be in our "vital interests" to have those
companies nationalized by either or both the Mideast governments and our own? Should we allow
Henry Kissinger, because of his long tutelage with the
Rockefellers, to deal with this for us as a technical
problem, or are there profound differences of interest
between the majority of Americans and the Rockefellers? Aside from the fact that I think those answers
should be affirmative, it remains that without the
devil theory, and in a time of economic travail, it will
be no easy matter to deny the relevance of such
questions. The Nixon Doctrine was formulated as if
you could have your Cold War cake and eat it too—
make peace with the commies and still operate on the
basis of a national fear. It will become increasingly
apparent that this will not wash either at home or
with our "friends" abroad, including those who were
the most reactionary (and hence most reliable), as
evidenced by the "betrayal" in the oil boycott by
the very Saudi Arabians we had installed in power.

chapter 3

ROCKEFELLER'S CORPORATE DIPLOMACY

To a naive citizen, one alternate basis for a foreign policy would be to have a much reduced foreign presence—to drastically lower military support commitment and other external meddling. If the Cold War is over, let's cut out the $100 billion spent on "defense," increase foreign aid through the UN "without strings," and let the world's people choose their own way. This would leave the multinational companies high and dry without the U.S. military machine or threatened aid cuts as an obstacle to nationalization, it would also cost U.S. taxpayers less and free substantial money for economic development. But we are still a long way from this alternative, and the question persists: If the U.S. is no longer "in the world" to stop communism and shore up free-world governments, then what are we in the world for? Kissinger would have it that we are there to build a new structure of stability, a new order of peace, and new multipolar understandings and mechanisms. Which is all well and good, but the question "toward what end?," as Kissinger concedes, is still very relevant: ". . . in the field of foreign policy, we will never be able to contribute to building a stable and creative world order unless we first form some conception of it."[1]

In my own personal conception of a "world order," I do not want the multinational corporations to be, as they now aspire in their propaganda, a new United Nations rising above petty national interest. In fact, casting my one vote, I don't even want them in the new world order. That is my view of my vital interests. It is undoubtedly not Kissinger's. But, the fog machine of the Kissinger-Nixon Doctrine with its language of "building for peace" or "to realize the creative possibilities of a pluralistic world" is aimed at denying that such a question even exists. Stability, pluralism, and peace in the current world, might all prevail through skillful diplomacy and great power machinations, and the overwhelming majority of the human race could be increasingly miserable, including a good chunk of us in the developed countries as well. There are different kinds of peace, different arrangements of stability; and the unposed, but decisive question of the Kissinger-Nixon Doctrine is "who has power?"

The fact is, that notwithstanding the Nixon Doctrine or de-escalation in Vietnam, the U.S. is very much in the world. It consumes a vastly disproportionate share of the world's resources, and its corporations make basic decisions for people from the suburbs of Tehran to those of Bangkok. Since this is the case, we must ask ourselves: "Are we in the world in ways that are good for Americans, and which Americans?" and "Are these ways good for non-Americans, and which ones?"

On his first full day in office, Nixon initiated his foreign policy by asking one American, Nelson Rockefeller, to head up a task force on Latin America to formulate the basis for a new approach to that area. According to Henry Brandon, of the London

Sunday Times,* Kissinger had suggested, prior to taking his new job, that Rockefeller be involved in some way.[2] It was a natural suggestion since Kissinger had been Nelson's top foreign-policy adviser in that year's primary campaign as well as for the preceding twelve years. That the Rockefeller-Kissinger relationship has been especially close—politically and personally—has been noted by all of Kissinger's biographers. Most recently, Bernard and Marvin Kalb referred to Rockefeller as one of Kissinger's "closest friends."[3] And of course his wife Nancy McGinnis still works for the Rockefeller Foundation. The Kalbs' account has Kissinger consulting with Nelson Rockefeller on virtually every major decision in his political life since they began their association in 1950. At that time Kissinger was director of Rockefeller's Special Studies Project. In his last Rockefeller report Kissinger asserted that "the willingness to engage in nuclear war when necessary is part of the price of our freedom."[4] As the Kalbs note, it was "in keeping with Rockefeller's slogan of 'a bomb shelter in every house.' "[5] Such hard-line views were to surface once again in Rockefeller's report on Latin America, undertaken for the Nixon administration at Kissinger's urging.

To a nontechnical expert, it might seem that a Rockefeller would not be the best person to make

---

* Brandon was Kissinger's confidant until it was discovered that Kissinger had ordered his phone bugged.

a neutral report; and, indeed, the government of Peru would not let his team in (nor did Venezuela, Chile, or naturally, Cuba). But, one has to understand that there exists a language, developed by those who work in the foreign-policy establishment, to discuss world politics without ever mentioning any crude facts of economic penetration or exploitation, lest this become useful to enemies of that policy (as with an earlier Eisenhower admission that we were in Southeast Asia for the resources). The Rockefeller trip was besieged by rock throwers denouncing him as an agent of imperialism, but that charge was simply not allowed to come up in Brookings Institute or Rockefeller Foundation studies.

It was in that spirit of avoidance that Nelson, in reporting to Nixon, mentioned the unfortunate Peru affair:

> As everyone knows, the mission encountered difficulties. The new military government of Peru stated that our visit would be "inconvenient" and requested indefinite postponement. This action was the result of a specific incident, growing out of the dispute between the United States and Peru over fishing rights and expropriation of oil fields, but it was unrelated to our mission.[6]

Perhaps everyone does not know that it was International Petroleum Company, Ltd., a Rockefeller-related subsidiary of Standard Oil of New Jersey, that was being nationalized in Peru,[7] and the historical actions of that company were not in any conceivable sense "unrelated" to popular opposition "to our mission."

Throughout the same report Rockefeller speaks for "we" Americans, which is the practice of the elite group that makes "our" foreign policy. The fact is that the vast majority of these high-level officials are people who before public life are trained to work for and service the needs of the multinational corporations and banks, either as corporate lawyers or executives. In those capacities they have become experts on the problems encountered by America's corporations abroad—it is their job to smooth the way—and yet we are expected to believe that that perspective is simply dropped when it comes time to formulate foreign policy.

We either have to believe that it is of no consequence to a man's thinking that he plays such a professional role in corporate life or, what is more likely, that he assumes no conflict of interest between said corporations and "those of America." One does not have to believe in sinister conspiracy theories to note that Kissinger is one of a long line of representatives of Eastern corporate "concern" for world affairs. More recently, former Secretary Rogers had his Wall Street base, as does John N. Irwin II, who has been Kissingers' second in command. It was Irwin who was sent to Peru in 1969, before he was Undersecretary, to persuade that government not to nationalize Standard Oil. But Irwin is not a mere pawn of Standard. Before becoming Undersecretary, he was made a director of the IBM World Trade Corporation (he just happens to be former IBM president Thomas Watson's son-in-law) and the Rockefeller-Astor United States Trust Company.

Now, if my old neighborhood stickball team wanted a free junket to Paris to try out for the Olympics, and I was Undersecretary of State, I'd give them a hand. I cannot accept the idea that the "training" and prior "role" played by an Irwin would not fundamentally affect his view of what "our" national interests are. If they don't, where does he get his view? Informal polling up and down Connecticut Avenue, or reading the President's mail? I am not referring here to questions of special-interest favoritism, of the kind rampant in the Nixon administration—*I mean his world view:* Are multinationals good for people? Should they be nationalized? Is private property sacred? Do banks perform honorable and necessary economic functions? Corporate lawyers and defense braintrusters for millionaire foundations do have assumptions about these questions.

I believe that the presence of the multinational corporations in the world is very much an issue of American foreign policy which the rest of us should be debating. Hence I feel the need to focus attention on their connection with our "vital interests." If this is a gauche departure from think-tank practice and "rational" discussion of strategy, it may also be a reflection of a bias more widespread in America than Kissinger would like to think—that the corporations are not neutral, disinterested good guys. In fact, that potential for isolationism which he finds so frightening is probably not in any sense an indifference to world humanity, but rather an old-fashioned populist hostility to, and suspicion of, the world-wide activity of the big corporations which ends up costing a lot for the rest of us.

It was mindboggling to me that I could not find one reference to the multinational corporations in a Brookings Institute briefing for the incoming President, when the rise of their economic activity in the sixties was one of the most startling new factors on the world scene. It illustrated an implicit acceptance of the propaganda image of the multinational as "non-political," and therefore outside of partisan debate. But a lot has changed since 1969—we have had the ITT and Watergate scandals as well as the so-called energy crisis. And we now know that the Nixon administration was very much involved with the multinationals and their needs as it formed policy, even though the braintrusters at Brookings weren't writing about it.

On the contrary, the Nixon Doctrine was conceived in order for America to "remain committed" and the government to be able to act when the vital interests of the multinational companies were threatened. Nixon was involved intimately with ITT's problems, one of which was staying in Chile; and his "stable order of peace" must have been intended to preclude the nationalization of such interests. If this was not the case, then the government was even more schizophrenic than it appears. Why should the President spend so much time servicing even the petty needs of the corporations, but leave out their basic concerns in the formulation of "foreign-policy structures"?

Certainly these concerns were taken into consideration in the Rockefeller mission reports which begin with the aim of finding ways to "stabilize" America's involvement in Latin America and conclude with stern prescriptions for upping the arms and aid to the military and police (at least the ones which were on our side). The staff for that report, coming as it did largely out of the Rockefeller Foundation, must have been made up of people close to Kissinger's thinking. And it is interesting, for all of the new perceptions about international communism being multipolar and the need for a détente with China, that the eight million people of Cuba appear in the Rockefeller report to be as great a menace as ever: ". . . young people were being drawn to Cuba in never-diminishing numbers, for indoctrination and for instruction in the arts of propaganda, the skills of subversion and the tactics of terror."[8] Our interests in Latin America, for the time being, have a heavier priority than those in Asia; and the Nixon Doctrine, as Chile sadly shows, is not about to allow a Marxist revolution in the hemisphere even though the official Cold War is over.

> The subversive capabilities of these communist forces are increasing throughout the hemisphere. The inflation, urban terrorism, racial strife, overcrowding, poverty, violence and rural insurgency are all among

the weapons available to the enemies of the systems
of the free nations of the Western Hemisphere. . . .
The seriousness of these factors when exploited by
covert communist forces is not fully recognized in the
United States.[9]

What the Rockefeller report, and the subsequent
policies pursued by the Nixon government made
clear was that the struggle for power was not over at
all—it was just in its newer "differentiated form."

Indeed, it was argued by Rockefeller and Kissinger
that overextension and overcommitment throughout
the world had made it difficult to intervene where it
was more necessary, and Latin America was judged
one of those more necessary places. It mattered not
that Allende believed in Social Democracy and Con-
stitutionalism, but rather that he was going after the
American companies. He was certainly no agent of a
foreign power, and was not even accused of having
designs on other nations, least of all the U.S. But he
was in a country that had a good deal of U.S. corporate investment, and he was moving against that. So
the U.S. moved against him, using all of the weapons
of subversion and economic control available to it,
from CIA meddling in Chilean labor unions to blocking World Bank loans.

It is simply not possible to put any other construction on the operation of the Kissinger-Nixon Doctrine
as regards Chile. And the obvious conclusion is that
there is an economic basis to the notion of stability
which it contains. It wants to retain an American role

or initiative in a world that accepts the activities of multinational corporations as part of their vision of stability and peace.

Until the recent Senate investigations of the multi-nationals, it was possible to think that the above statements very much exaggerated their political as well as economic importance to American society and to the world. But there is now an abundance of evidence demonstrating that it is very difficult to overestimate that influence. The multinationals employ some of the best minds of our time—be they those of accountants, college professors, or PR writers, to conceal or put the best coloration on virtually every facet of their operations. But the distance between the PR image of these corporations and their key role as units of control becomes increasingly evident with each week's headlines.

That some corporations, in particular the large multinationals, do feel that they have vital political interests is now a matter of common record, thanks to the new disclosure laws, congressional investigations, and the lawsuits by groups like Common Cause and Nader's Raiders. According to a *New York Times* analysis of that data, financial and banking executives were the largest group of donors to Nixon's re-election campaign with over four million dollars in gifts. Oil company executives were the second most generous with almost one and a half million dollars changing hands. The drug and pharmaceutical industry ranked third with over a million.[10] All three of those categories of business activity depend on government decisions, and we now possess a long list of detailed examples of their manipulation of government regulatory bodies, import quotas, approval of foreign trade deals, tax write-offs, and, of course, pressure on foreign governments.

While it may be true that some of the corporate rich made campaign donations for altruistic or personal reasons, the pattern was clear. Nixon got twenty-five million dollars more than his opponent because he stood for a businessman's view of the system. The Rockefellers must have had to swallow hard but they came up with hundreds of thousands of dollars for this "rival."

Money that did not come to Nixon because of the special needs of a corporation came as a result of his being identified with the larger class interests of the corporate world. As *Fortune* magazine stated:

> The C.R.P. fund raisers deny that they applied improper pressures to obtain contributions. According to one who solicited some of the largest gifts, the technique used was to stress the importance of Nixon's reelection to the future of the country and the free-enterprise system.[11]

Since the existence of such class consciousness on the part of corporate executives has been systematically downplayed by academic experts on American society, it is worth quoting *Fortune*'s survey of business attitudes toward campaign contributions: "Many contributors, particularly the largest ones, are moved by philosophic or ideological concerns, or by desire to preserve or strengthen the political or economic systems."[12]

They offer the example of Ray Kroc, Chairman of the McDonald's hamburger chain, who gave Nixon $255,000 on the suggestion of Maurice Stans that he, "aid the President's re-election as a means of supporting the free-enterprise system that had made all his success possible."[13]

The "free-enterprise" system responded favorably once again with Nixon's veto of the minimum-wage bill a year later, which would have raised McDonald's operating costs considerably, given their miserably low pay scale.

Other companies are interested in preventing government regulation of their business in other ways. As *Fortune* cited:

> In the words of the chief Washington lobbyist of a major corporation: "It's not so much that we want something done *for* us as that we want to avoid having something done *to* us." Most such giving in recent years has been a form of insurance—an investment in government that is favorably disposed toward business in general, and an effort to assure future good will towards the giver's company in particular.[14]

In recent years the corporate-executive function has increasingly become a political one, even more than an organizational or scientific one, and for that reason one of the fastest tracks to corporate power is now through one of the prestigious law schools. Indeed the role of the corporate lawyer, whether in-house or in a related independent firm, is absolutely decisive to the functioning of the large multinational companies.

The Watergate hearings focused national attention on the dominant role of the corporate lawyers as fund-raisers, lobbyists, fixers, negotiators, or power brokers. They were everywhere doing everything—getting tax favors, blocking suits, passing money to politicians, and, most importantly, building alliances between the corporate and governmental bureaucracies.

None of this was extraneous to Nixon, who had lived smack in the middle of the corporate legal world. His real apprenticeship for the Presidency was not as a brash rightist Congressman, or an unsettled and politically insecure Vice President, but rather as a member of the corporate law firm of Mudge, Stern, Baldwin and Todd, which was reorganized to include him and later John Mitchell, making it one of the top ten corporate law firms. He was also a director of six different companies during this period, involving railroads, mutual funds, and insurance, all of which demanded a large amount of government contact. In 1968 as a Presidential candidate he sent a confidential letter to the Wall Street elite attacking the Johnson administration bureaucrats who "sought wide-sweeping new regulatory powers over the mutual fund industry . . ."[15]

When he went off to be President, Pepsico president Donald M. Kendall replaced him as the director of the four mutual funds. And it was Kendall who later emerged as one of Nixon's most trusted business advisers, sticking with him to the end.

The Pepsico case is typical of government-multinational relationship. The rise of Pepsico simply would not have happened had not Kendall and his fellow executives and lawyers been able to thread their way through the maze of government regulation and power peddling. He took a troubled one-product company through the path of conglomerate mergers and spreading multinational business, all of which involved government cooperation at various levels. If Kendall has an executive skill, it lies in his ability to move between the worlds of business and government to secure the needs of his corporation. His friendship with Nixon dates back to the days of the Vice-Presidency. One of the great moments in Pepsi's history occurred when Richard Nixon debated Nikita Khrushchev in that Moscow kitchen and included a plug for Pepsi as the carrier of all that is good in the American way of life. When he was out of work after the defeat in the 1962 California election, Kendall offered him a job at Pepsico. But Elmer Bobst, of Warner-Lambert, had already persuaded Nixon to enter into partnership in a newly reorganized law firm. As *Business Week* reported, Pepsico became his second client after Warner-Lambert. The favor has been returned on many occasions through United States government assistance in Pepsico's foreign adventures, including the deal with the Soviets where Pepsi became the sole exporter of United States soft drinks to Russia in return for locking up the vodka import business to this country. As with so many of Kendall's other deals, this required United States government approval, and it was always forthcoming. But Kendall speaks for even larger interests than Pepsico's, and in this other work President Nixon was also most helpful. As the Chairman of the Emergency Committee for American Trade, which serves as a pressure group for the interests of the multinational corporations, Kendall has been the most visible spokesman for their interests at congressional committee sessions. In particular, he led the fight against the Burke-Hartke Bill, which aimed at cutting out the tax loopholes that exist for the benefit of the multinationals' overseas operations. The Nixon administration marshaled all of its forces against that AFL-CIO sponsored bill, and offered a substitute for it which retained the deferred profit schemes that allow the multinationals to avoid paying taxes on earnings they leave abroad with their affiliates. Donald Kendall was most grateful for Nixon's efforts and must have felt that they justified his earlier support of an unemployed politician when he observed: "It would be very difficult for the multinationals to get a better bill than the one the administration offers."[16]

Pepsico was not the only multinational among Nixon's former clients who contributed heavily to his campaign. In "Wall Street to Watergate," a special report published by the North American Congress on Latin America (NACLA),* an independent research group, examples were compiled:

---

* NACLA publishes a monthly report and research pamphlets on U.S. involvement in the Third World. They can be contacted at P.O. Box 226; Berkeley, CA., 94701 or P.O. Box 57; Cathedral Station; New York, N.Y., 10025.

1. El Paso Natural Gas, while battling an antitrust suit, had paid the law firm $770,000 in legal fees (1961–67). Two months after Mitchell took office, the suit was dropped.

2. Warner-Lambert Pharmaceutical's 1970 merger with the Parke-Davis drug company pushed their annual sales over the $1 billion mark. The Justice Department's antitrust chief, Richard McLaren, had tried to block the merger; but after Attorney General Mitchell disqualified himself "in order to avoid any possibility or appearance of conflict of interest," Deputy Attorney General Richard Kleindienst stepped in to rule in favor of the merger.

3. ITT also retained Mudge, Rose from 1969 to 1971 to do legal work for its subsidiaries Continental Baking Company and Hartford Fire Insurance Company. Justice antitrust chief, Richard McLaren, tried to block it. Finally, after Mitchell again removed himself from the official decision, Kleindienst made a settlement which allowed ITT to keep the insurance company. McLaren was finally forced to leave his antitrust position.

4. Cargill, Inc., is one of the largest privately held multinational companies engaged in grain trading and other agricultural ventures. It was a major participant in the Soviet wheat sale. In December 1971, President Nixon appointed Cargill Vice-President William Pearce to be his deputy special representative for trade negotiations. In 1963, the government had found Cargill guilty of manipulating the wheat futures market. The Department of Agriculture's Commodity Exchange Authority, after seven years finally decided to place Cargill's top officers on probation for their crime. The ineffectiveness of the action was highlighted later when a Cargill trader admitted to a house subcommittee that he could not remember whether he was still on probation.[17]

The list of major campaign contributors to Nixon indicates a high concentration of gifts from rich corporate executives and an obvious "business perspective." Twenty-eight major contributors alone gave $10,255,867, as disclosed by the Committee to Re-elect the President, which meant that together they contributed more than one-sixth of the funds that financed the campaign. That group included Chicago insurance tycoon, W. Clement Stone, who gave 2.1 million dollars; Richard Mellon Scaife, an heir to the Mellon industrial and banking fortune (Gulf Oil, Aluminum Company of America, Mellon National Bank), who gave a million dollars; and John A. Mulcahy, president of one of Pfizer Pharmaceuticals subsidiaries, who gave almost six hundred thousand. Three dairy-producer groups came up with another $422,500 which resulted in support for higher milk prices. Five members of the Rockefeller family contributed $310,000 and two dozen trucking firms gave an equivalent amount. Another big contributor was the late Arthur K. Watson, former chairman of IBM International, who gave $300,000.[18]

There were smaller contributions like J. Paul Getty's $122,000 and Howard Hughes' $150,000 (that we know about).

The oil industry was additionally represented by Robert Kleberg of the King Ranch. He gave $100,000. Otto N. Miller of Standard of California gave $50,000, and Armand Hammer of Occidental Petroleum, $46,000. Elmer H. Bobst, honorary Chairman of Warner-Lambert, gave $100,000.

The *Los Angeles Times* summarized the list as follows:

> Manufacturing of all types, including heavy industry, shipbuilding, food products and rubber products, led the list with 29 entries, followed by oil companies with 11 donors, banking and investments with 10 and motion pictures and entertainment with six.[19]

While it is possible to make too much of the specific *quid pro quos* of such contributions, they are very much present. In the case of Ashland Oil, an illegal $100,000 corporate gift was recently admitted, for which they received the administration's blessing for a deal with Iran to produce and market oil.[20] Iran, in turn, is a pillar of strength in the Nixon Doctrine program for the Middle East. And it was the Harsco Corporation, of which Nixon was formerly a director, which received a fifty-million-dollar contract to modify and re-equip the tank arsenal of that same country. It does seem that the Nixon administration was more generous than past administrations with specific favors to select interest groups, and it is that excess which shocked the press. But the more important point is that it is a business perspective which guides the American government, and that the key officials who make our policy, starting with the President, have, more often than not, worked the corporate side of the street in civilian life.

The consciousness of the business community was, until recently, accepted as that of the country, and in the days of the Cold War even big labor somehow fitted its needs into all that. The coziness of the business-government relationship came to be challenged only in the new post–Cold War days of economic trouble, when old arrangements were suddenly suspect. For all of his overreaching, Nixon had been basically following the patterns of his predecessors. Indeed, the Senate Watergate Committee came up with substantial, though less publicized, evidence of Humphrey's corporate campaign funding and connections.

Gerald Ford, through his long apprenticeship in the Congress, is even more directly linked with corporate lobbyists than was Nixon, more closely perhaps than any previous U.S. President. This was clear from the first day of his administration. As *The New York Times* reported: "President Ford's circle of friends from the business community includes several of Washington's most powerful corporate lobbyists, some of whom are helping shape his Administration during the transitional period."[21]

Three of his "closest and most trusted friends," according to the *Times,* are William G. Whyte, vice-president at U.S. Steel; Rodney W. Markley, Jr., Ford Motor Company's top Washington lobbyist; and Bryce N. Harlow, Proctor & Gamble's chief Washington representative. Harlow was a White House counselor to Nixon and "played a major role in writing the last three Republican party platforms while he was employed by Proctor & Gamble."[22] Other close friends are Stark Ritchie, who has gained some attention as chief general counsel of the American Petroleum

Institute, and John F. Mills of the Tobacco Institute, Inc. And the list of lobbyist friends of the new President seems endless: "Many of the businessmen close to Mr. Ford pointed out that the new President had an extraordinary number of business friends."[23] His appointment of Nelson Rockefeller as Vice President is a further indication of Ford's commitment to the corporate perspective and the continuance of the dominance of the foreign-policy establishment.

The degree of Ford's involvement with Washington corporate lobbyists represents merely an expansion of the link between government and big business that has shaped the recent practices of the Presidency.

This continuity of corporate-government partnership was revealed in clearest detail in the opening of the history of oil company negotiations by the Senate Foreign Relations Subcommittee on Multinational Corporations during the energy crisis. The figure caught in the middle was John J. McCloy, perhaps the most respected member of that group of corporate lawyers specializing in high-level government contact. The following account by William Moore of the *San Francisco Chronicle* conveys the changing temper of the times, and gives an insight into how business-government relations were conducted even before we had Richard Nixon to kick around:

> The five senators were essentially questioning the propriety of the secret relationships that existed between the highest levels of government and a consortium of 29 oil companies McCloy has been representing as an attorney.

Over the years, as McCloy testified, he prided himself on bringing assorted private interests and government officials together.

"It has been a perfectly natural way to get things done," McCloy told the *Chronicle*.

. . . . Among other posts, McCloy was once chief US Arms Control Negotiator and the postwar high commissioner in Germany.

Richard Rovere, the political writer, once described him as the "cornerstone" of The Establishment in America.

. . . . Matter-of-factly, he related how he suggested in 1961 to President Kennedy "who sought my views" that it might be necessary for the major oil companies to take some sort of concerted action to negotiate with the Arab oil nations which together with some non-Arab nations had just banded together in their own organization to negotiate as a bloc.

. . . . Attorney General Robert Kennedy, after talking with McCloy, had agreed to let the oil men negotiate as a group with the Arabs without fear of antitrust action.

. . . . He added, almost casually, that nothing was ever put in writing. He himself just passed the word along about the arrangement to each succeeding attorney general, he said.

. . . . Senator Stuart Symington, one of the Senate's most powerful members, angrily started questioning McCloy:

. . . . "At what point," pursued Symington, his face reddening, "does the taxpayer, who's putting up money for defense spending that is supposed to protect things like our foreign investments, like oil, at what point does the taxpayer have something to say about what the price of oil should be."[24]

The entire transcript of those Senate hearings should be made the basis of teaching high-school civics, for it reveals more about the actual day-to-day functioning of government than all of the precepts about division of powers and limited government. Power in the modern context of massive budgets and bureaucracies has to do with access, and what McCloy was revealing was not only the incredible access of top corporate lawyers like himself to the government, but that those lawyers provided the basic perceptions and continuity for the government: It was he who notified subsequent Attorney Generals about the "arrangement" which was in violation of the law but acceptable because business found it "perfectly natural." For a decade, under three elected Presidents of presumably varying philosophies and representing different constituencies, the oil consortium continued to make policy in the Middle East. It was they, and not the elected officials, who negotiated about what was really important there to our foreign policy: the oil, its price, and its disposition.

There have always been two foreign policies; one which we all debate about and vote on and the other which affects the vital interests of the multi-nationals. Both use the government as a funnel, but in retrospect the issues we deal with "democratically" through the elective process are far less consequential for our lives than those the multinationals deal with through their lawyers.

While the American people were arguing about "defense," which was supposed to have to do with protecting us against communist aggression, Symington (as head of the Armed Services Committee) knew all along it had to do with "things like our foreign investments, like oil." What caused Symington's face to redden were the increasing *public* revelations that the private companies we had been protecting were not working for the best interests of the American public, and that his constituents now knew it.

McCloy's way of bringing government and business together had been perfectly acceptable to those in power, including Symington and even "liberals" like Bobby Kennedy, in the days when the American public bought the bit about the corporations and public having the same interests. If that were true then there would have been no scandal in 1974 in having the oil companies bargain with the Arabs for our oil needs. The fact that they were not bargaining for "our needs" but rather their own, or indeed that the two can be different, has only very recently been admitted into the American political consciousness.

When, as the *San Francisco Chronicle* reported, "John J. McCloy said he couldn't help but feel that he and the ideas he stood for were somehow on trial,"[25] he was not speaking of his personal ideas alone but rather those which had formed the basic part of the American Cold War consensus.

For all its rhetoric about new "creative forms" and "we must not be prisoners of strategy," the Kissinger-Nixon Doctrine was incapable of coming up with a new consensus for support of the prerogatives of American corporations. On the contrary, it was left nakedly reliant on the old corporate prerogatives while at the same moment it was shedding the ideology of anticommunism. In an exercise in mindlessness that must have been rationalized by some expectation of public stupidity, the Nixon administration went on prattling about how "our vital interests" were menaced by the communists, while it eagerly expanded trade with those communists (even facilitating the sale of items like wheat which played havoc with the domestic economy). The needs of the corporations for "stability" in the world economy and "trade" with the communists had come into conflict with the government's need for anticommunism as a unifier of the American people. But Nixon, ever the workhorse, went on vainly with the gambit hoping that somehow, with the adroit use of TV and domestic repression à la the "enemies" list, nobody would notice or dare to report the obvious.

chapter 4

THE LIMITS OF LIBERALISM

There is little reason to doubt that the men who make our foreign policy, from the President on down, have internalized a positive view of the large corporations and that they are in that sense sincere when they assume that the continuous expansion of corporate activity is good not only for America but also the world. Such sincerity is easily sustained in the insular world they inhabit, shielded as it is from troublesome countertheory and fact. If one is permitted to assume the general beneficence of corporate activity as an unquestioned given, then charges of economic imperialism can be dismissed as so much misguided polemic—the ravings of radical hysterics and naive environmentalists. Thus we have the rhetoric of Bobby Kennedy in response to the radicalism of Indonesian students in 1962:

> I am a representative of the United States here. What is it that you mean by monopolistic capitalism? What is it that defines that description in the United States? You said it in a derogatory sense. What is it that meets the description in the United States? What do you mean by monopolistic capitalism?[1]

I first came across that quote in the preface to Paul Sweezy's and Paul Baran's well-documented and reasoned essay "Monopoly Capital" published in 1966 by their own Monthly Review Press, a small publishing venture that had persisted somehow through the bleakest years of the Cold War. When I interviewed Bobby Kennedy a year later, I discovered that although by that time he had more doubts on this question, he had still not troubled to delve into any of the serious literature available. For all of the impeccable academic credentials of a Sweezy (former Harvard professor) and Baran (Stanford), they did not inhabit the world of top establishment politics. Bobby's education had been left to the likes of W. W. Rostow and Arthur Schlesinger, Jr., whose primary contribution to the ideological debates of their time was the attempt to prove that there was no need for such debate, all big issues having been already resolved within the structure of our society.

But the history of the past ten years since Baran and Sweezy wrote their book has shown their analysis to be the more relevant one. Yes, Virginia, there clearly is a monopoly capitalism and it is increasingly expansive, wasteful, and global in dimension. The phenomenal rise of the multinational corporation in this period is now widely conceded in the business press, and even the vaguest sense of historical accuracy would require an admission that the small band of Marxist economists were alone in demonstrating any capacity to predict its development. As Baran and others tried to tell us, the corporate growth we have witnessed is not accidental but rather flows from the very nature of modern capitalism. The workings of the large multinational corporations provide the basic dynamic of our modern political economy. But if one turns to mainstream academic social scientists for some insight into all this, the literature is still disappointingly thin.

One legacy of the Cold War that still persists—for

all the new stirrings of the past few years—is the continuance of a dominant pattern of intellectual work that is in no serious way troubling to those who have power in the society. Despite past student attempts to restructure the universities, the bulk of the new investigations, research, and reportage has come not from leading academicians, but from muckraking journalists, environmentalist crusaders, a few mostly nontenured teachers, and disparate bands of poorly paid, left-wing collective researchers and "underground" snoopers. The framework of the social sciences remains compartmentalized and irrelevantly detailed; there is little capacity or willingness to develop any "grand theories" or "ideologies" which might make sense out of the welter of scandalous data unearthed by the muckrakers. But without such an ordering of data into some meaningful pattern, we become overwhelmed and demoralized by the shotgun effect of innumerable horror tales. It all seems to point nowhere except that some bad people are once again in power, and we must wearily try once again to eject them from office and vote in some "cleaner" or more decent types.

The problems which we are discussing in this book did not find their origin in the special trickiness of Richard Nixon, nor have they disappeared with him. They are, more accurately, a manifestation of the structure and class content of power in America, and, in particular, in the relationship of the economic sector to the political sector. The milk price scandal, wherein a lobby got from the executive

and Congress the milk price it wanted, occurred under Democrats and Republicans alike, as did the
machinations of ITT and, of course, those of the oil
lobby. These scandals were not scandals at all, if the
word implies the unusual, they are a more expected
and normal part of the American governmental process than the "pluralistic democratic society" which
political scientists have been celebrating all of these
years.

The unreality of academic work seems particularly
skewed when we turn to the field of economics for
some insight into the problems raised in the preceding chapters. What we find is that the world of multinational corporations and banks, which control markets and countries with the backing of the U.S.
government, is dismissed by avoidance. It is simply
not mentioned except in some of the unconventional
writings of a John Kenneth Galbraith or a few Senate antitrust economists. The Marxist writers like
Sweezy and Magdoff, who center their analysis on
such corporations, have been kept on the fringes of
academic life. But more recently a growing number of younger economists, particularly the group
around URPE (Union of Radical Political Economists) have begun to reassert the relevance of a Marxist analysis. Indeed, even the venerable American
Economic Association has been forced by their pressure to elect Stanford's Jack Gurley, a Marxist, vice-
president and to add America's leading Marxist
economist, Paul Sweezy, to their executive committee.
But one suspects this is tokenism. Of course the business schools which train corporate executives devote

more attention to the real world of the multinationals. But for the vast majority who take (often
required) introductory college economics to learn
something about why they couldn't get gasoline that
morning or why their privately endowed college was
going out of business because of a super-costly fuel
bill, it is still the fairy-tale world of Paul Samuelson's
introductory text.

There, one can still discover the innocent delights
of the competitive economy, supply and demand, and
marginal productivity, not to mention the old efficient resource-allocation-through-profit-maximization
gambit. But the interrelation of corporate, political,
and economic power is dismissed as a preoccupation
of the New Leftists who are not serious academics,
which is the Alice-in-Wonderland way of saying they
are *too* serious.

In recent years such textbook accounts have been
"modernized" to keep their place in what is barely a
competitive market, since the consumers (students)
have no choice. But they have made concessions with
skimpy sections on "women," "race," "Third World,"
etc. All of which preserves the idea that problems
such as racism or imperialism are marginal ones, and
that the important thing is to stick with the old,
tried and true analysis.

One reason for the poverty of economic theory is
that this "science" has been compartmentalized to
exclude the study of social forces most vital to economic decision-making. To approach economics as
somehow separate from politics, sociology, and psy-
chology simply does not work for the modern eco-

nomic order, and probably didn't even for the simpler one of Adam Smith's day. Yet economic science still attempts to deal with the "firm" as if it is not an entity of political economy, even though the basic decisions of that company may rest most heavily on political considerations; for example, defense contracts, taxation, government regulation, or, certainly in the case of multinationals, the threat of nationalization.

But the weird skewing of modern economics goes beyond leaving out the important "noneconomic" variables. For even the "economy" that is dealt with is unreal. Amazingly enough we still have thousands of very bright individuals called economists teaching hundreds of thousands of clever students about the workings of an economic world that both groups know has no greater approximation to reality than a game of parcheesi. The justification for this work, which can get quite sophisticated and involve complex mathematical models and computer analyses, is that, even though the basic competition model of the economy is wrong, results based on that model are somehow relevant to the real world. Just why this absurdity should be true is never explained other than by the fact that the people with power in the profession want it to be true because it is what they know, their stock in trade, so to speak; and to study something else would mean beginning all over again. And that is something which middle-aged men with power and security are universally loath to do. So an economic church has developed to preserve the dogma.

Meanwhile, the world has been lurching rapidly away from such fantasies. It is no longer possible to get a "man in the street" poll that shows that a majority of the people still believe in consumer "sovereignty," or that corporations do not have decisive political power, or that they allocate resources rationally. In a recent introduction to one of the few books that deals with the fact of the concentration of economic power, a grand old man of the profession, Gardiner Means, addressed himself to the obscurity of his fellow economists. He did so in the context of a conversation he was having with a visiting Martian, who, perplexed by what he could see as a tourist of the American economy, turned unhappily to those who are paid to inform on this subject:

[Means]: Did you read P. A. Samuelson's *Economics?*

[the man from Mars]: Yes, I was told it was the textbook most widely used in the colleges.

[Means]: Then you noticed that in the first 458 pages of the eighth edition, 1970, Samuelson gives one page each to the "Imperfections of Competition," to "The Evil of Monopoly" and "The Curse of Bigness," but it is not until page 459 that he starts his fifty-page analysis of imperfections and monopoly. Up to this point the description of the working of the economy is in terms of classical competition, and at no point are the imperfections built into his stereotype model of the workings of the economy as a whole. Rather, for the economy as a whole he gives the classical stereotype model, modified by Keynesian theory.

Actually we don't have any textbook that starts off by saying that the classical principles do not explain the workings of the modern economy because so little is produced under conditions of classical competition. The truth is that in practically no industry is price determined by supply and demand; almost nowhere in industry is production pushed to the point where marginal cost approximates price. Even the concept of clearing the market has ceased to apply to commodities and services except in agriculture, which provides less than three per cent of the gross national product, and in a few raw materials with an international market like lead or zinc. The typical methods of marketing involve advertising rivalry and administered prices, neither of which can occur under classical competition.[2]

The importance of the theory of production being pushed to the point where marginal cost approximates price is that it justifies capitalist economic activity as the most efficient allocation of resources. If there were no advertising and no oligopolies or monopolies, there would be some truth to that judgment, although one of Marx's contributions was to demonstrate the inherent instability of even that model. But why quibble—the model doesn't exist. We live in a world of "advertising rivalry and administered prices," where there is a great deal of waste, resources are not efficiently allocated, and corporations have power in the political as well as the economic realm. In this world consumption does not equal utility, either for the individual or the aggregate of society. To understand the extent of corporate power, we have to study how corporations make decisions and appraise that social effect.

The notion of "imperfections" in the market is no longer valid if the imperfections are, in fact, the central characteristics of the system. As an illustration, Samuelson in his most recent edition makes exactly four references to advertising that are noted in the index—"It would be humanly impossible," he writes, "to attempt to create perfect competition by law. The problem is one of achieving reasonably effective workable competition."[3] But if in fact demand is induced by advertising and other manipulations, then there is nothing efficient about allocating resources to meet that demand. And if prices are set administratively by a few firms who control the market, then their decisions about output have nothing to do with marginal efficiency. To pretend that they do is to provide a moral justification for a system that is itself a lie, and yet this is what the "neutrality" of economic science comes down to.

Another cover of Samuelson's is the rubric of the "mixed economy" which is supposed to combine the blessings of the free-market economy with those of government regulation through input of social goals like full employment, greater income equality, and pollution control. He calls this mishmash "political economy," while carefully avoiding any investigation of the political power of corporations, the intertwining of corporate bureaucracies and their government counterpart, defense contracting, government underwriting of private corporate research, etc. It is as if the government is a neutral computer, swinging into action only when certain indexes such as the unemployment rate reach a given point. In Samuelson's view, "the citizenry through their government step

in with expenditures . . ."⁴ A more accurate version
would be: The corporations through their lobbyists
and through their government step in with expenditures. One of the rude lessons of Watergate is that
the modern corporation does not exist primarily as
a market phenomenon. It is rather an administrator
of political economic power and its key decisions are
made by tax lawyers, lobbyists, advertising agencies,
marketing specialists, and cost accountants—with
market "forces" most often a lesser and more mal-
leable variable than the others in the sociopolitical
environment.

In his ninth edition, published in 1973, Samuelson
added a "Winds of Change" section which even had
a grand four pages (out of nine hundred) on Karl
Marx, with a total of eleven lines on the content of
Marx's economic writings. He states: "It is a scandal
that, until recently, even majors in economics were
taught nothing of Karl Marx except that he was an
unsound fellow," but, "This was not out of intimida-
tion by the plutocratic interests . . ." only because
economists like Keynes thought Marx "sterile and
dull."⁵ Has Samuelson never heard of the Cold War,
of anticommunism, of the firing of Marxist professors? Or is he so inured to irrelevance that he cannot
make even the most elementary connections between
social cause and effect? There were plenty of budding
American Marxist economists at the advent of the
Cold War, and the general hysteria of that period
certainly had something to do with their disappear-
ance. Doesn't Samuelson know of Paul Sweezy's troubles with Harvard, or Marcuse's with Brandeis? These

events occurred in his own Cambridge neighborhood, as did Harvard's firing of economics professor Sam Bowles only last year. To admit to any of this would undermine the pretense of neutrality and science, so dear to the privilege of academic economics. So while in the ninth edition he makes painful concessions to the existence of some new imperfections in the market, sex and race discrimination are discovered, some doubt is entertained about sheer growth in the GNP, and there is some allusion to the environment and the quality of life—let anyone suggest that all of this warrants a thorough revamping of economic science, let alone the economic order itself, and the patience of this neutral scientist wears very thin. Those radical New Leftists who suggest this are no longer simply proponents of a contrary view, but rather carriers of a disease. And more respectable critics of establishment thinking, like Galbraith, are unwitting symps. Lest I be accused of New Left hyperbole, I will quote Samuelson in full on this point:

> Galbraith does provide a ware that is in great effective demand: a critique in viewpoint against the prevailing orthodoxy in economics—against the "conventional wisdom," in his phrase, the "received learning," in Veblen's. His criticism cannot itself kill. But it acts like a virus, softening the way for more deadly critiques on the part of the New Left and its professional radical economists.[6]

It's the commie virus of Cold War days. In comparison to Samuelson, Galbraith appears a source of clarity and realism.

Galbraith writes a lot and is sometimes on every

side of every question, which makes it difficult to sort
out his central logic. But despite the occasional bril-
liance and refreshing relevance of his analysis it seems
to be based on a fallacy developed in his first book,
*American Capitalism: The Concept of Countervail-
ing Power,* where he asserted that big business bureaucracies were countervailed by big union and big
government bureaucracies. He has, through all his
subsequent writings, been obsessed with this notion
of the commonality yet rivalry of these various bureaucracies. In his first book they were in relatively
equal, and therefore stable relation. In *The Affluent
Society,* the business bureaucracy had gotten out of
hand and government services were impoverished.
Lately he has come to feel that the big business bureaucracy (planned sector) is out of balance with what
remains of the market sector. It ends up a hopeless
mess because Galbraith cannot get beyond his preoccupation with bureaucracy to isolate other forces
in the society. By focusing on the bureaucracies, "life
of its own," he denies that bureaucracies, whatever
their ingrown or entrenched attributes, exist to serve
larger social forces (economic classes, social group-
ings, national forces). The business bureaucracy serves
a class, and, to the degree that it controls government,
which is evidently a very high degree, it can get the
government bureaucracy to serve the interests of that
class, rather than the majority of the people.

Galbraith's refusal to deal forthrightly with the
question of "for whom," robs all of his categories
and terms of their real meaning. He finds, for ex-

ample, that "planning" on the part of the big companies produces some undesirable results such as pollution, or wasted resources, or, his latest, "uneven development," and calls for supplementary planning by the government. He ends with a theory of imperfect planning in much the same way as the neoclassical economists end with a theory of imperfect competition. Neither view starts from what is, but rather from what the writer hopes is the case.

After all this, we are still left with the fact that the large, primarily multinational corporations are the key units of our social life. These units exist and grow because they have political power, and if their growth is now judged a menace (and both Samuelson and Galbraith at points imply this may be the case) then these units must have their power taken from them and different ways of organizing economic activity must be created. But while these units may be socially undesirable, they continue to grow because they do benefit some. They serve certain class interests at the expense of others, and part of the job of the social scientist is to help clarify what those class interests are. Marx's seminal contribution was to put this matter of class interest and class struggle at the center of historical change—a proposition which Galbraith and Samuelson simply ignore in their hasty efforts to dismiss Marx.

Perhaps the most relevant of Marx's insights for our time was his examination of what he called the contradiction between socialized production and private ownership. He pointed out that the historical function of capitalism was to amass capital and labor into new, large, socialized units of production, replacing the small and independent handicraft artisans. As opposed to the craftsman who owned the tools of his production, the new economic stage necessitated costly and complex tools, which increasingly were made productive only by pooling larger numbers of workers to operate them. It was a process which involved the elimination of those older modes of production (such as self-employed craftsmen), and the ushering in of a new work force that was disenfranchised from the means of production. As we witness today with a GM assembly line, production is now in a basic way "socialized," in that one part cannot function without the other. A high degree of planning is required and human labor comes to be viewed as an input to production rather than as a creative or controlling agent. But while a broad mass of the people are socialized into the production of goods as workers, they do not "own" or "control" the productive process. They do not determine the purposes of production. These goals remain private whether they are goals of "growth," or "profit." Claims that workers or "people" control production based on "democratic ownership of stocks" or "consumer sovereignty" are simply rationalizations for the concentration of power in the hands of a few.

A growing recognition of this conflict between socialized production and private ownership is indicated by the corporate spokesmen, who are now forced to talk of a "corporate conscience" in response to environmentalists and others who talk of misplanning and social misuse of production.

Marx was writing before the rise of the large corporation, which only gained real strength at the turn of the century after his death. But he had glimpses of such future configurations. Describing the "centralization of capital" as opposed to the simple expansion of the individual capitalist firm through natural productive growth, he stated: "The laws of the centralization of capital, or of the attraction of capital by capital, cannot be developed here. A brief hint at a few facts must suffice."[7]

But this "brief hint" is unfortunately more to the point than the bulk of contemporary economic analysis. Since most people know Marx only through derogatory or condescending snatches in elementary textbooks, I would indulge the reader's patience with a lengthier quote from the concluding pages of volume one of *Das Kapital,* and remind them that it was written over a hundred years ago. Yet judge if one can currently find many more accurate descriptions of the new global capitalism of the multinational corporations:

> As soon as this process of transformation has sufficiently decomposed the old society from top to bottom, as soon as the labourers are turned into proletarians, their means of labour into capital, as soon as the capitalist mode of production stands on its own feet, then the further socialization of labour and further transformation of the land and other means of production into socially exploited and, therefore, com-

mon means of production, as well as the further expropriation of private proprietors, takes a new form. *That which is now to be expropriated is no longer the labourer working for himself, but the capitalist exploiting many labourers.* This expropriation is accomplished by the action of the immanent laws of capitalistic production itself, by the centralization of capital. *One capitalist always kills many.* Hand in hand with this centralization, or this expropriation of many capitalists by few, develop, on an ever-extending scale, the cooperative form of the labour-process, the conscious technical application of science, the methodical cultivation of the soil, the transformation of the instruments of labour into instruments of labour only usable in common, the economising of all means of production by their use as the means of production of combined socialized labour, *the entanglement of all peoples in the net of the world-market, and with this, the international character of the capitalistic regime.*[8]

Marx died before the international character of capitalism was established and it remained for Lenin to extend the analysis. But professional economists have been even more cursory in their treatment of Lenin's ideas. For example, Paul Samuelson writes that Lenin simply predicted "wrong." He devotes a single paragraph in his text to summarizing Lenin's writings, lumping them together with those of Rosa Luxemburg, apparently to save space:

As the twentieth century developed, Marxian writers like Rosa Luxemburg and V. I. Lenin added the view that mature capitalist countries will engage in *imperialistic exploitation* of colonial peoples. Capitalism's prosperity will depend on exploiting oil, bauxite, iron ore, uranium, and other natural resources. To keep up purchasing power at home and avoid mass unemployment, and to stave off falling rates of profit from accumulation at home, mature capitalist nations will indulge in much foreign investment and cold-war expenditures. So it is argued.[9]

Amazingly enough, the above is offered by Samuelson as *not* corresponding to the "facts" of "modern reality."

In light of the fact that the new writers of the managerial-revolution school often claim that the divorce of the stockholder from corporate power is a refutation of Marxism-Leninism, it is perhaps useful to quote the following from Lenin which anticipates Galbraith by some fifty years:

> In other words, the old capitalism, the capitalism of free competition with its indispensable regulator, the Stock Exchange, is passing away. A new capitalism has come to take its place, bearing obvious features of something transient, a mixture of free competition and monopoly. The question naturally arises: *to what* is this new capitalism "passing"? But the bourgeois scholars are afraid to raise the question.[10]

In attempting to answer that question Lenin developed his theory of imperialism as the highest stage of capitalism. This theory anticipated not only the further economic penetration of the Third World, building on Marx's idea of "the net of the world market," but also the rise of newer capitalist institutions, such as the multinational corporation, and the shift from the export of commodities to the export of capital. The five "basic features" of imperialism which he outlined have proved a nearly flawless description of the modern global economy even as it is currently described in *Fortune* magazine. These are, to quote Lenin:

1. The concentration of production and capital has developed to such a high stage that it has created monopolies which play a decisive role in economic life;

2. The merging of bank capital with industrial capital, and the creation, on the basis of this "finance capital," of a financial oligarchy;

3. The export of capital as distinguished from the export of commodities acquires exceptional importance;

4. The formation of international monopolist combines which share the world among themselves;

5. The territorial division of the whole world among the biggest capitalist powers is completed.[11]

Perhaps in part because of Lenin's impact upon modern history, point five has been somewhat hindered. There have been revolutions against imperialism and in large sectors of the world they have been successful. As to the other points, they unfortunately seem to have been predicted all too accurately, as the following chapters will indicate.

part two

U.S.
CORPORATIONS
IN THE
WORLD ECONOMY

chapter 5

CITIZENS OF THE WORLD

According to the image pushed by the PR literature, the multinational corporations are the new citizens of the world, transcending the petty restraints of nation and culture. They are modern capitalism's answer to Karl Marx's International. In a more mundane and accurate sense, they are simply big companies which engage in production using local labor within more than one country, and are, in fact, with very few exceptions, national corporations in the explicit sense that the parent organization owns or controls the affiliates and is situated in a "home" nation. Most of the top management and board of directors come from that nation and it is that nation's government and army which provide the multinational with the protection or muscle to operate internationally. It is also the case that about 60 percent of the largest of such corporations are American-owned with the ownership of the rest divided among a few Western European capitalist powers and Japan.

The multinationals are very much a sixties phenomenon. During that decade they experienced an average annual rate of increase in revenue of 10 percent. While *Fortune* magazine predicts this increase will drop to 5 to 7 percent per annum, which is substantial enough, they maintain: "Those rates imply that by 1980 a value of U.S. direct investments abroad should range between $160 billion and $180 billion and should produce between $400 billion and $450 billion worth of goods and services."[1] In 1972, *Fortune* predicted that the $10 billion in profit recorded by the multinationals for that year "could easily

double" by 1980. That was before the incredible
profits of the oil companies in the energy crisis.

This foreign investment is important to more than
a minority of U.S. companies. The term "multinational" is commonly used to imply that there are
some companies like ITT that are obviously international in scope, but that such companies exist as a
separate category of American corporate life and that
their problems are also distinct. *But virtually every
top American corporation is multinational.* Indeed,
the rankings of the top multinational corporations are
almost identical to the *Fortune* rankings of the top
U.S. manufacturing concerns. The same corporations
and banks which dominate the domestic American
economy (along with a lesser number of European
and Japanese multinationals) dominate the world
economy. It is Lenin's thesis of imperialism as the
highest stage of capitalism come spectacularly true. In
the past fifteen years the American economy has become intertwined with the world economy in a
dramatically new way, and it is no longer possible to
deal with wages, pricing, shortages, or resource allocation as merely domestic issues. Corporate capitalism
is indeed creating an international order but its executives and major stockholders are the only voting
citizens.

That these executive-citizens are in some sense
international, their primary allegiance being to the
company even more than the home country, was
ilustrated by the response of Franklin E. Agnew,
senior vice-president of H. J. Heinz, to the AFL-

CIO-initiated Burke-Hartke bill: "If Congress passed this bill, Heinz would give serious thought to discorporating in the U.S. and moving its headquarters to another country."[2] And what could be more American than H. J. Heinz catsup?

According to a recent UN study, a corporation such as Heinz receives almost 50 percent of its profits from its foreign operations. The directors of U.S. Steel have not displayed similar candor but these issues must be of equal concern to them, given that 62 percent of their profits in 1971 came from foreign operations. And this foreign economic activity is even a key to the survival of General Motors, with only one-fifth of its profit coming from overseas, Goodyear with one-third, or IBM with half.[3]

It is also generally understood that foreign profit figures probably do not reflect the effect of the true profit derived from foreign operations. Sidney Robbins, a leading academic expert on such matters, stated: "There is enormous potential for saving on taxes by adjusting prices within the corporate structure—so-called transfer prices."[4] This is a fancy way of saying that recorded profits can be held down simply by raising the prices charged by affiliates. But this dubious practice is limited by the fact that the companies need the foreign earnings. As Robert Stobaugh of the Harvard Business School observed: "These companies have come to depend on their foreign earnings to help them pay their corporate dividends. As a result they bring home a great deal of money."[5] As Marxists like Harry Magdoff have pointed out, the

question is not whether these profits earned abroad
are a big percentage of the American gross national
product, but rather what they represent to the largest
corporations which control the American economy.[6]
There is little doubt of their dependency on foreign
earnings no matter which figures are used for profit
calculation.

The UN has calculated that for the period of 1965–
1968 the average return on book investment of U.S.
companies was 7.9 percent from investments in the
developed countries and a much larger 17.5 percent
in developing countries, a large part of that being the
whopping profits (over 40 percent) in the oil industry.[7]

According to the UN, the gap between money
invested in the Third World and that taken out increased substantially in the seventies. *By 1970 almost
four billion more dollars were taken out of the developing countries as income on past investments than
were being put back into them in the form of new investments.*[8] (That four billion dollars from the
developing world looms big in the balance-of-payments situation.) This amount is twice what the U.S.
government offered as economic aid to the developing
countries, and destroys the myth of the U.S. support-
ing the Third World. On the contrary, it is obvious
that U.S. aid permits the entry of U.S. corporations,
allowing them to take out an amount greater than
they and the U.S. government put in.

During the sixties a clear pattern of mutual interest
developed between the multinationals and the U.S.

military machine. The latter protected U.S. investments by maintaining military bases, assistance programs, and sabotage teams throughout the world. This required a major outlay of dollars abroad, thereby straining America's international financial position. But foreign earnings of U.S. corporations repatriated to the U.S. offset these military expenditures. Secretary of State Rogers, in his 1972 annual report, praised the multinationals for balancing our international trade books:

> A recent survey by the Department of Commerce of the operations of the larger multinational companies reveals how impressive the range of their activities is. The survey covers the operations of 298 U.S. based companies with about 5,200 foreign affiliates. The years covered are 1966 through 1970. In this period the sales of foreign affiliates of these firms grew at an annual rate of about 13 percent, nearly twice as fast as the sales of the parent companies. A large part of total U.S. foreign trade, and of the growth in trade, was associated with these companies. Of the $27 billion increase in U.S. exports and imports from 1966 to 1970, $12 billion was attributed to such companies. In 1970 these companies accounted for 51 percent of all U.S. exports and 34 percent of total U.S. imports. Furthermore, the trade surplus associated with these firms rose from $5.3 billion in 1966 to $7.6 billion in 1970, while the surplus on total U.S. trade fell from $3.5 billion to $1.9 billion.[9]

In this period, Secretary Rogers went on to observe, sales made by foreign affiliates of corporations amounted to about one-third of their domestic sales. This is impressive, given that these companies are

among the main corporations in our domestic economic life. Secretary Rogers reiterated the President's
position that "the U.S. Government, together with
American business, is taking measures over the long
term to help protect U.S. investment abroad."[10] One
weapon he mentions is that of World Bank loans:

> Specifically, it is our policy that when a country
> expropriates a significant U.S. interest without mak-
> ing reasonable provision for compensation, it should
> be presumed that the U.S. Government will neither
> extend new bilateral economic benefits to the ex-
> propriating country, nor support loans to that coun-
> try by international development banks . . .[11]

He was not providing this assurance because the
multinationals are good taxpayers deserving of such
solicitation. It is well known that the tax laws are
rigged in favor of overseas corporate activities: U.S.
taxes on their profits are not paid by foreign affiliates
until those profits are remitted to the U.S. If they are
reinvested for greater foreign expansion they are tax
free. These corporations also receive a dollar-per-
dollar credit on the foreign taxes they pay, which
brings their normal domestic tax rate of 48 percent
down to around 34 percent for foreign operations.[12]
The oil companies of course get to apply the oil
depletion allowance to their foreign operations,
which are called "branches" rather than "affiliates," so
as to qualify for charging the cost of foreign oil
exploration against U.S. income.

It's a good deal if one views the world as a truffle
patch to be rummaged around in. The Department of

Commerce estimates that the parents of multinationals supply only about 15 percent of their affiliates' funds.[13] The rest are generated from retained earnings and overseas borrowing. With this minimal commitment of their own funds and substantial use of those of other countries they have developed a commanding position.

The totality of U.S. foreign assets abroad and the profits they generate are of too large proportions not to be a major factor in any administration's thinking. In 1950 these assets totaled $31.5 billion and by 1970 they were $170 billion.[14] As *Fortune* stated: "The largest single factor in this growth has been our direct investment abroad—essentially the investments of the U.S.-based multinational companies. Since 1950 the book value of these investments has increased by about $75 billion."[15] *In a real sense then there is another U.S. out there.* Even Secretary Rogers conceded:

> . . . U.S. foreign investors have been hyperbolically characterized as the "world's third greatest power." Tensions are generated when U.S.-controlled MNC's take over established industries and concentrate in the advanced sectors of the economy. Developing countries, too, worry about the large size of MNC's in relation to their own economies.[16]

He should have added that an increasing number of Americans do too.

The multinationals are an agency for disenfranchising people by making social and political decisions for them and the economic activity of these units most often dwarfs that of the countries in which they operate. As a recent UN survey held:

> . . . the general conclusion that many multinational corporations are bigger than a large number of entire national economies remains valid. Thus, the value-added by each of the top ten multinational corporations in 1971 was in excess of $3 billion—or greater than the gross national product of over 80 countries.[17]

This means that all of the planning, resource allocation, and savings decisions of any one of those countries is of less significance on the world level than any one of the top ten multinationals. It also is a measure of the power of such corporations relative to that of many of their host countries. Their ability to withhold investments or access to markets is a weapon in gaining concessions. The multinational form of operation is designed to play one country against another until the most "favorable conditions" for business are found.

The multinationals account for one-fifth of the world's GNP (excluding centrally planned economies), giving some indication of their control over investment and resource allocation. Since the multinationals are not responsible for the wider range of social services and other responsibilities of national governments (e.g., military expenditures, education, health), their one-fifth is really a far more flexible and decisive sector of economic activity.

The production of such corporations overseas is now far more important than the international trade of the world's countries. In the words of the UN survey, international production "measured by the sales of foreign affiliates of multinational corporations, has surpassed trade as the main vehicle of international economic exchange. It is estimated that international production reached approximately $330 billion in 1971."[18]

The multinational corporation is not merely a mechanism for the penetration of advanced economies into poorer ones. It also enables one capitalist power to move into the economic life of another. One fiction holds that there is really no net penetration since U.S. investment in Europe is canceled out by European investment in the U.S. While it is true that quantitatively European investment in the U.S. is about the same as the U.S. investment in Europe, the form of that investment is fundamentally different. European investment is 70 percent portfolio investment in U.S. stocks and bonds.[19] The presence of European multinationals in the U.S., producing goods here, is, in the words of the UN survey, "not as yet significant." On the other hand, fully 80 percent of U.S. investment in Europe is direct investment through American-owned affiliates.[20] Stockholders do not normally have power over the investment and allocation decisions of corporations. But the home offices of multinationals very definitely control such decision-making on the part of their affiliates, from the selection of top management to investment, pricing, and sales decisions. Within the French economy General Motors makes decisions about wages, employment, and profit, whereas a French stockholder in General Motors makes no decisions at all.

The total foreign operations of American multinationals are basically financed by foreigners and do not represent a net addition to the capital stock available to foreign economies for their own development. As the UN survey stated:

> In 1971, United States multinational corporations generated an outflow of capital of $4.8 billion for direct investment abroad and an inflow of approximately $9 billion in interest, dividends, royalties and management fees. Furthermore, given the practice of extensive local borrowing, their control of overseas assets is substantially higher than the book value of long-term equity and debt held abroad.[21]

This statement makes a shambles of the image of American capital pouring out to a capital-hungry world to aid in economic development. The truth is, America is making money abroad without laying out new capital.

The degree of penetration by multinationals varies. In Japan, for example, foreign activity accounts for only a few percentage points of total fixed assets and sales, due to very restrictive policies by the host government; whereas Canada has been taken over in a very real sense. Multinational corporations, mostly U.S.-owned, control 60 percent of Canadian manufacturing and 65 percent of mining and smelting output.[22]

But the influence of multinational corporations is

underestimated even by such aggregate figures, for their activity tends to be concentrated in the most vital economic sectors. The UN survey summarized this:

> There is a high concentration in a fairly small number of industrial sectors characterized by fast growth, export-orientation and high technology, sectors which are also regarded as key sectors by the host countries.[23]

This same report states that foreign firms operating in the developed countries own between 50–100 percent of high-technology industries. This would include the oil-refining industry, chemicals, computers, electronics, and transportation machinery. For example, U.S. multinationals control three-fifths of the food, tobacco, oil-refining, metal-manufacturing, instrument-engineering, computer, and technical-manufacturing industries in the United Kingdom. They control half of the petroleum industry of Belgium, and these same U.S. multinationals own 80 percent of computers and electronic data processing equipment industries in the European community.[24]

The flow of direct foreign investment to the developed countries increased by an average annual rate of 9 percent throughout the sixties, and the stock of such corporations in most cases increased at a rate faster than the local gross domestic product.[25]

About one-third of direct foreign investment is in the developing market economies, which is more significant given that these countries only produce about one-sixth of the world's gross domestic product. The pattern of this investment is shifting away from that of the plantation agriculture of United Fruit fame to the manufacturing and service sector. It should also be added that U.S. multinationals' affiliates in developed countries operate in economies which draw heavily on Third World resources. Computers in France owned by IBM are dependent upon Algerian and Iranian oil for energy inputs.

Because of the fragility of Third World economies, this growth of multinationals means an even greater disenfranchisement than in stronger economies. The multinationals can make life-and-death decisions by deciding to close up shop, cut production, or transfer part of an operation to an affiliate in another country. Third World countries are aware that if they seek to nationalize an affiliate, this action will affect loans from the developed countries and international banks, as well as frighten other companies into cutting production or increasing the flow of capital out of the country. For that reason partial nationalization in an otherwise capitalist economy seems inevitably doomed as a means of controlling corporate activity.

Mexico provides a startling example of this. Long celebrated for the early moves of her revolution to gain control over petroleum and other resources in key sectors, Mexico is now very much under the thumb of foreign investors, despite all sorts of regulations which were supposed to prevent that. The UN concluded that,

In Mexico, among middle- and large-sized firms, weighted average foreign participation reached 45 percent in 1970. Foreign participation in the output of Mexican manufacturing industries, however, reached 100 percent in rubber products and transportation materials, and a weighted share of more than 75 percent in industrial chemicals and tobacco in 1970.[26]

Of the five hundred largest manufacturing firms in Brazil, 37 percent of total assets were controlled by foreign affiliates. Brazil represents a "new frontier" of vast resources, and figures high on the list of countries deemed important by the Nixon Doctrine. In Central America fully 30 percent of the total output of manufacturing is by foreign affiliates.[27] This U.S. penetration of Latin America is not simply a reflection of historic relations but rather suggests that that area is perceived as a key sphere of influence in the current plans of U.S. corporations and the government.

This investment would not have been possible were it not for a vast network of U.S.-sponsored banking credits, import subsidization plans, loans, advisors, CIA coups, and, of course, the threat of U.S. military intervention, all of which established a "sound business environment." In this sense, then, it is important to recognize two results of the multinational presence in Latin America that run directly counter to the stated aims of American foreign policy for that area as enunciated by John Kennedy's Alliance for Progress. One such aim was the emergence of a new middle class of entrepreneurs and managers native to the area who would form the vital political element for a flourishing democracy. The other was the inducement of a pattern of balanced and sustained economic growth along the lines of more egalitarian income distribution as basic to stability. The multinationals have played havoc with both goals.

The multinationals select out from the local population a new elite trained to rise, not in the nation-state, but within the parent company. This new management grouping has loyalties that are supranational. Indeed, they often fully expect to be transferred at some point to another affiliate, or even to the parent companies if their stars are really rising. In a basic way, their interests are in conflict with those of the native bourgeoisie, whose future, for better or worse, is rooted not in the fate of a multinational corporation but in their own country's economy and their little piece of it. As a leading Latin America specialist put it in an article in *Foreign Affairs:*

> A significant part of the national bourgeoisie is being transformed into a private transnational technocracy, losing legitimacy as part of a national ruling class. . . . this process not only prevents the formation of a national entrepreneurial class, but also limits and erodes the middle classes generally (including intellec-lectuals, scientists and technocrats) and even creates privileged and underprivileged sectors within the working class, adding another serious difficulty to the creation of a strong labor movement.[28]

The writer, Osvaldo Sunkel, a UN economist, notes that the role of the multinational is quite dramatic:

These contribute significantly to shaping the nature
and operation of the economy, society and policy, a
kind of "fifth column" as it were. Thus, the concept
of "dependencía" links the postwar evolution of
capitalism internationally to the discriminatory nature of the local process of development, as we know
it. Access to the means and benefits of development
is selective; rather than spreading them the process
tends to ensure a self-reinforcing accumulation of
privilege for special groups as well as the continued
existence of a marginal class . . . this approach considers the capitalist system as a whole, as a global
international system, within which national economies . . . constitute sub-systems.[29]

So, on a global level, these subsystems accustom
people to inequity through sufficient infusions of the
waste-economy, commodity culture to those select
portions of local populations which are in the service
of the multinationals. These include lawyers, small
producers, and others who are dependent for their
livelihood on the corporations, while not being directly on their payrolls. The issue, then, becomes
one of national survival, and so it is not surprising
that during the sixties, as the role of the multinational expanded dramatically in Latin America, non-
political generals often popped up on the side of
nationalization and anti-imperialism, for national
honor was indeed at stake. Foreign-owned companies
could not be trusted with a state's sovereignty.

A legitimate enough fear. What parent-company
executive, sitting in New York, is ever really going
to worry about being sensitive to the development
needs of one of those eighty countries who have a

lower total GNP than his company's sales? He is in the home office precisely to move business around from less to more profitable affiliates, from country to country, depending upon the profit climate. Such executives are citizens of the world, just like they are citizens of the U.S., which is precisely why their companies are now under attack in the Third World.

chapter 6

THE
GROWTH
MANIA

Penetration and waste by multinationals within the world economy are inevitable as long as the allocation of resources is based on the profit motive. It is the business of multinational corporations to waste resources as quickly as they can in the most socially irresponsible or nonresponsive fashion possible, simply because *profit through growth* is their raison d'être. We may try to monitor them governmentally, we may implore them to shape up—to which they may respond by initiating community-oriented recycling programs or putting longhairs and folk rock in their commercials—but they cannot stop this pattern of wasteful growth. They would, in fact, become inefficient units. Attempting to pursue any other central goal would involve a fundamentally different reward system within the corporation. If the multinationals started promoting people for effectively curtailing sales, or discouraging socially unnecessary new products it would create a psychologically untenable situation for their executives. They become multinational precisely to expand their technology, capital, patents, marketing techniques, and managerial skills outside their national boundaries.

The real institutional significance of the corporation in modern capitalist society cannot be restricted to legal definitions, the calculations of cost accountants, or the intricate mathematical models of supply-and-demand behavior so dear to economists. It has much more to do with basic power in a real world which knows no separation of politics from economics, of psychological fantasy from marketing, or of culture from sales. Power to make profit means power to manipulate not only labor and capital, but also expectations, fears, and the political process. It means being able to control resources, government regulation and the evolving pattern of family life. Economic decision-making in dynamic capitalist society exists within a social superstructure that is itself changing and whose change can be manipulated. There is no such thing as a "business climate." There is only the social climate within which business forces are principle actors. It is for these reasons that the efforts of writers of economics textbooks to ignore the facts of corporate political power have been in absurd contradiction to daily events.

The modern corporation has grown in size because size is related to power, be it through lobbying in Washington, buying off local inspectors, national marketing campaigns, brand name identification, or large investment in research and development. In one sense the large American company was always multinational, the U.S. (and Canada) being at one point a series of fragmented nations or states of people. The large corporations united those disparate communities. They were able to organize the movement of labor across a continent, to accumulate and invest large pools of capital, to shape American educational institutions to meet the needs of the new technology, and of course, to gain the compliance of local and federal government in facilitating interstate corporate activity.

An obvious conclusion can be drawn from the

record of corporate activity: growth has been basic to survival and profitability, and this growth has fed inevitably on itself. There are, to be sure, small and profitable corporations that have not grown, just as there are ones which grew very large and collapsed. But such cases are the exceptions which prove the rule. The fact is, that after a century of corporate activity, as Professor Douglas Dowd recently noted:

> The 500 largest industrial corporations in 1972 controlled 65 per cent of the *sales* of all industrial companies, 75 per cent of their total *profits* and 75 per cent of total industrial *employment*.[1]

Clearly the activities of those top five hundred corporations, together with the top financial institutions, are *the* American economy, and not the hundreds of thousands of little firms left competing for the crumbs.

Until the Second World War, and even well into the fifties, growth occurred primarily within the "continental" United States and was therefore thought somehow to be national as opposed to imperial. In contrast with European capitalism, desperate for expansion beyond its limited terrain, the American variety had an empire to conquer before it crossed any oceans. By employing the fiction that the North American continent was somehow "ours" by "eminent domain" we could wantonly plunder the treasures of Indians and Mexicans without appearing imperialistic. And if we wasted this treasure in a subsequent orgy of consumerism it was perceived con-

veniently as no one's business but our own. But by
the 1960s, having skimmed the cream of these resources, American corporations began to break the
bounds of nation and move on to rake over the rest
of the world's surface. A whole generation of American professor-apologists were caught by surprise by
this development. They had made their living during
the Cold War by arguing brilliantly that the United
States, despite mounting evidence to the contrary,
could not be imperialistic since most of its economic
activity was "internal."

Third World radicals within the United States first
gave the lie to this notion by reconstructing domestic
American history as one of colonization, slavery, and
racism. Paralleling their strident challenge in the
early sixties, the peace movement focused attention
on the defense contracts of a handful of corporations,
and the "military-industrial complex" began to be
perceived by a majority of Americans as a grim but
prosperous reality. In turn, the environmentalists
found that "waste," "pollution," and "safety" were
problems originating from an economic base going
back to the corporations—corporations which were, in
fact, making profits from their contribution to these
problems.

It was only with the seventies and the major strains
on the economy that organized labor began a process
of separation from its Cold War marriage of convenience to big business. The runaway shops of the
multinationals threatened the bureaucratic security
of top labor. The AFL-CIO has been moved to de-

nunciations of the multinational corporations, particularly as they affect domestic unemployment and wage rates. A recent report entitled "U.S. Multinationals—the Dimming of America," prepared by the AFL-CIO Maritime Trades Department Executive Board, sounds the alarm in terms that make this author's prose seem conservative:

> Proud countries are losing the power to shape their own destinies, to guide their economies, to collect their taxes, to better the lives of their people. They are increasingly at the mercy of stateless, soulless, anonymous multinational corporations.[2]

The AFL-CIO view that the corporations have embarked upon the path of uncontrolled growth is supported by a study prepared by the American Management Association. The study is based on interviews with top multinational executives who stressed the necessity of growth to modern manufacturing success:

> Most companies interviewed emphasized that merely "being a profitable company" is not good enough in today's world of international business. A small but profitable company cannot possibly face up to the competition offered by giant multinational companies. The desire to survive is what motivates the small companies to grow. Profit is important to these companies, but to ensure a continuous flow of reasonable profits over the long run, they must grow. And if they are to grow, expansion of manufacturing and sales abroad is a must, because either the home market is not big enough or the domestic economy is not growing fast enough to sustain the company's desired growth.[3]

This need of a company to grow faster than its national economy is equally true for the European multinationals. As the chairman of the London-based Dunlop Corporation stated (to the AMA):

> It is one of Dunlop's objectives to double net after-tax profits during the next ten years and to increase its average rate of return on net funds employed to a minimum of 17.5 percent per annum before interest and taxation. The U.K. market—from which some 40 percent of the company's earnings arise—is not growing fast enough to achieve the desired level of growth. The company has to get less dependent on the U.K. economy, and so it is seeking greater tire market shares, together with investment opportunities in faster-growth areas overseas. Dunlop is making forecasts of areas that have a better than average growth potential over the next decade, and from this will evolve a geographic pattern of development consistent with an acceptable level of political and economic risk.[4]

There is a fatalism to all this. These corporations are indeed creatures of growth. In the final analysis they survive only by growing faster than the economies in which they sit. Thus they remain the centers of action, sapping capital and talent which would otherwise go to more dynamic competitors. In the corporate world, accumulation and salesmanship are the name of the game and if you want to play another one, say "zero growth," you need different players.

As the senior vice-president of a large American drug company told the AMA survey:

The desire of this company is to be a growth company. The responsibility of this management is to make the company grow both here and abroad, to be a growth company. Otherwise we are not doing our job.[5]

We do not possess a full explanation as to why managers like the one above are so wedded to the goals of profit and growth, but we do know that despite what celebrants of the managerial revolution claim, they are not simply motivated by bureaucratic imperatives, psychological whim, infantile love of bigness, or executive privilege—all of which are factors but hardly basic ones. Managers are responding to a more serious set of signals which cannot be brushed aside by reference to the fact that many stockholders are without power over the corporation. To begin with, some do have power. Owners of big blocks of stock, be they families, banks, insurance companies, or mutual funds, are very concerned about the profit and growth picture; and it is they who determine the makeup of boards of directors, who in turn hire or fire the top executives. Nor is it easy to gauge the extent of such control over corporate life. As a recent news item indicates, this control has been subject to considerable concealment: "Two Senators charged yesterday that there is 'a massive coverup' of the extent to which stockholdings in large corporations are concentrated 'in the hands of very few institutional investors, especially banks.' "[6]

The Senators, Metcalf (Democrat, Montana) and Muskie (Democrat, Maine) each chair a government operations subcommittee. They issued a joint report of their committees, listing such coverup efforts by banks, which used anonymous "nominee" or "street name" accounts that actually belonged to the bank. For example, one-fourth of the stock (a controlling interest in almost every company) voted at the 1972 stockholders' meeting of Burlington Northern, an energy and transportation conglomerate, was held by four banks—Bankers Trust, Chase Manhattan, Bank of New York, and State Street.[7] "But Burlington Northern named none of the four banks in reports on its 30 largest stockholders filed in 1973 with the Interstate Commerce Commission and Securities and Exchange Commission."[8] In a perhaps more disturbing illustration of bank power it was revealed that Chase, Bankers Trust, and Bank of New York together held almost one-fourth of the stock in ABC and CBS. Chase rounded out this ownership of network stock with its holding of 4.5 percent of Metromedia.[9]

These banks may not interfere in the daily operations of the firms they own, but they certainly help set broad goals of growth and profit for the management teams. If these goals are not met, the management team will be replaced long before any public proxy fight, which would not be useful to the outgoing managers' reputations any more than to the banks'.

But, even if we accept, as John Kenneth Galbraith does, the image of growth as the goal of a "managerial revolution" divorced from ownership, retained earnings are a key to growth as well as management prestige and bonuses, and these must come out of profits.

Large stockholders generally share the commitment of managers to plow back earnings for growth as a way of avoiding taxation on current stock dividends. If the company grows they will be able to sell later with a lower capital gains tax. Both management and large investors have a common stake in growth to ensure long-run profit. John M. Blair, the former chief economist of the Senate Subcommittee on Antitrust and Monopoly, concluded from the Senate's data that the corporate goals of growth are in fact ensured by a predetermined profit as a percentage of investment. Decisions about output, sales effort, and prices are all aimed at ensuring that "necessary profit."

This settling on what Blair calls "targets of profit" —acceptable to stockholders, to the public through government taxation, and to host governments in the case of multinationals—shifts the emphasis of corporate management from short-term efficient use of resources to long-run growth in the market.

The setting of profit targets, by a company's administrators, is more a political decision than an old-fashioned economic one. It has to do with manipulating a host of social variables that have a political nexus or ultimate restraint in the form of taxation, regulation or nationalization. The phrase "what the market will bear" refers then to a larger political or social market rather than a narrow economic one.

The long-view target range of profits for large

oligopolistic corporations was found in a major
Brookings Institute study to be between 10 and 20
percent net return on capital.[10] These profit margins
are after taxes and, as Blair points out:

> To the extent that the leaders attain target rates, the
> corporation income tax is effectively transferred to
> the consumer. In terms of the time required to pay
> off their investment, General Motors and Du Pont
> seek to price their products in relation to costs in
> such a way as to yield an amount that would enable
> them to pay their corporate income taxes and recap-
> ture the stockholders' investment in only five years.[11]

It is a test of the political as well as economic power
of the five leading companies examined by John Blair
that they almost perfectly met their desired target
profit goals. As Blair concluded:

> Over the 16-year period (1953–1968) the success of
> the 5 leaders in meeting their profit objectives is little
> short of remarkable. As compared to its target return
> of 20 percent, the weighted average of General
> Motors actual rate of return on net worth was 20.2
> percent. As compared to its target of 8 percent, U.S.
> Steel averaged 8.4 percent. Of all the firms, Alcoa's
> profit rate experienced the widest year-to-year fluctua-
> tions, but its average of 9.5 percent compared closely
> to its objective of 10.0 percent. The company with
> the steadiest performance was Standard Oil of New
> Jersey, which matched its target of 12.0 percent with
> an average performance of 12.6 percent. The highest
> average return was recorded by Du Pont, whose
> earnings for the entire period averaged 22.2 percent
> as against its objective of 20.0 percent.[12]

This long-run stability of profits as a percentage of net worth persisted during a period which included two recessions and one rapid boom and occurred in splendid indifference to shifts in productivity, labor rates, and consumer demand. The "planning" involved was long-term and it permitted the companies, if not the larger society, to enjoy remarkable stability in their profit-making.

These companies, as long as they maintain their commanding market position, are not susceptible for their profits to the vicissitudes of general market forces. In 1954 and 1958, U.S. Steel's production dropped by more than 20 percent, but they were able to maintain their target profits by raising prices and, in fact, they exceeded their profit targets in both of these recessions.

The problems of oligopolistic leaders in maintaining these profits are complicated in recent years by increased foreign competition within the U.S. market and abroad. If import controls could be held and if foreign governments did not reciprocate by blocking U.S. products, there would be no problem. But in the recent period there has been growing domestic pressure for imports of such consumer items as the automobile, as well as imports by manufacturers of materials like steel. The penetration by foreign companies into the American market is a reflection of the increased strength and reliability of their home economies.

As the market, particularly in the sixties, became

increasingly a world-wide market, the oligopolies have been forced to attempt to duplicate the power they enjoyed domestically on an international level. They are thereby able to strike a blow at foreign competitors' penetration in the U.S. by competing with them in their home territories (as in the case of GM's Opel outselling Volkswagen in Germany) as well as obtain a power position in what is, in reality, more and more a homogeneous world market. In this context the imperative of growth becomes world-wide, as it was formerly national.

It is not surprising, then, to find that the oligopolistic leaders we have been discussing are all multinational corporations. General Motors operates in over twenty-one countries and Alcoa in twenty-eight.[13] U.S. Steel, the price leader in the domestic steel industry, receives 62 percent of its targeted earnings from its overseas affiliates, Standard of New Jersey over 50 percent, and Du Pont and General Motors close to 20 percent.[14]

But not only the leaders or price setters in the oligopolistic sectors receive high earnings abroad. Ford is in thirty countries and gets 24 percent of its profit abroad while "little" Chrysler with a mere $8 billion in sales is in twenty-six countries and also gets 24 percent of its earnings from the foreign market. So the delicate ballet of pricing and profit setting is increasingly a world-wide one.[15]

Since some economists have questioned the importance of profit-making as an incentive to overseas expansion, it might be helpful to quote an outspoken appraisal of this by the Union Carbide Corporation. After noting that many businesses are reticent about talking openly about profits for fear of adverse public reaction or "misunderstanding," they state:

> The primary motivation of American corporate investment, whether in the United States or abroad, necessarily is to earn a profit. Reasonable profit is completely and fundamentally essential to our democratic private enterprise system—it is in effect the "grease" that makes the wheels of industry turn. Without profit, new investment would cease and eventual closing down of industry would result.

> With reference to UCC particularly, net profit per share in 1971 was $2.61, or 5.2 percent on total sales value. Of this, UCC's international operations contributed 74¢ per share, or 28 percent of the total. This was a very significant contribution to our earnings, and certainly helped to support our domestic operations.[16]

To understand the desperation behind this desire for profit through foreign expansion it is necessary to look more closely at the nature of international competition which the new technology has brought about. It involves breaking with an older and lazier view of monopoly capitalism. In that view there was an assumption of limited space—a company invents something, secures a patent, creates a market. Because of economies of scale it expands to a commanding control of the market (or does so in concert with others) and then proceeds to milk the market for what it will bear, given various restraints of good will, pressure from labor unions, and possible government intervention. To this mix was added the warning that if things got out of hand and profits became too attractive there would be a danger of new companies starting up and attempting to capture part of the market. But it was assumed that the start-up costs of such entry would be quite high, if not prohibitive in many cases, due to the rigid structure of companies, the compartmentalization of knowledge, and the locking up of technology in patents.

But the modern economy is marked by a rapid turnover of technology, huge pools of surplus capital that must find an investment outlet, and conglomerates which enter by design into any area that is profitable. Those old assumptions about start-up costs become unrealistic. The modern company is under different restraints and impetuses.

Companies now make larger investments in research and development and the technological breakthroughs they bring don't stick around very long before new ones replace them. They have to be made into products and moved fast. This means being able to "scan" as wide a market as possible and to market products as fast as possible. An increasing volume of sales is the only answer to increasing research-and-development costs in a time when patents will not hold their earning power for long.

The conglomerate nature of many of the largest companies, as well as their ability to generate and borrow more and more capital, make the buying up of affiliates around the world a natural way of offsetting competition. And this international oligopolistic competition of the giants now moves very swiftly within the emerging world market.

This was revealed in the comments of the general manager of Hercules International to the AMA:

> I do not think that any company can let its competitor have a world position and itself be content with a national position. It is a kind of a threat to survival. This is a driving force that makes companies, if they think about it, think globally.[17]

as well as in reference of the executive vice-president of Ingersoll-Rand to: "a realization on our part that we might better compete forcefully with those fellows abroad than to try to defend ourselves here."[18]

Another aspect of the current growth economics is that these companies are churning up profits which they often do not want to report or pay taxes on. As one alternative, they reinvest it. Earnings of the U.S.-based multinationals abroad are not taxable until they are sent back to the mother country. Exaggerated depreciation allowances and unnecessary expansion and proliferation to other activities are logical outcomes of this pressure to retain earnings overseas. It is a process of waste that extends from building unneeded plants to padding executive expense accounts. It speaks to the conflict between social priorities as set by the U.S. government (presumably acting for its citizens by collecting taxes) and profit targets set by corporations, who undermine government programs by effectively withholding taxes through invented costs.

In a similar vein, in instances when foreign governments have attempted to prevent the repatriation of capital by multinational companies, the aim was presumably to turn it to some good local purpose. The government of Turkey, for example, tried to "freeze" or keep Pepsi Cola's profits in that country to be put to use there. Pepsico responded by taking over the local glass industry in Turkey with the "frozen" profits and began to export glass bottles to its other affiliates. When one of the Senators at the multinational hearings asked Pepsico's Kendall about this, Kendall replied: "We take the glass out of the plants that we have got an investment in in Turkey and sell it to a third country for hard currency and we get the hard currency; Turkey does not."[19]

The internal transfer of profits within these multinationals is almost beyond the ability of a small country to monitor.

It is this "being within the business environment" of a foreign country (rather than exporting to it) that is the key characteristic of multinational business. From that fact flows the power to manipulate governments, markets, and prices, to beat competitors and increase sales and profits. It is a power relationship rather than simply a trade one. And the multinationals themselves are quick to point out that they would prefer to have this power without going through all the difficulty of setting up plants, finding new managers, or learning languages or local customs, but that "penetration" is a requirement of doing business in the modern world economy.

The Chairman of Union Carbide echoed this need before that same Senate committee:

> We would prefer to serve foreign markets with exports from the United States. . . . [But] one of the things that our experience makes clear: if we do not respond, some other international competitor certainly will. . . . Because of this kind of economic competitive pressure which results from the normal industrial growth and development in foreign countries, companies like Union Carbide have found it necessary to invest in foreign manufacturing facilities.[20]

The new element in the rise of this competition was the rebuilding of other capitalist economies in the fifties, and it was this that made multinational expansion or direct foreign investment a necessity for the growth of these companies in the sixties. It's what Kendall had in mind when he said: "The day of the Marshall Plan approach is over. We once could afford the Marshall Plan. But we can't afford that kind of program today."[21] The same thought is, of course, prominent in the worldview of Henry Kissinger. The Marshall Plan had "done its work well" in preventing a socialist Europe and preserving a free environment, but its success had given rise to the new problem of rival capitalist powers.

In the neo-colonial era in which U.S. hegemony was a fact, U.S. companies could rely on exports, and, in any event, were still preoccupied with the domestic market. Now we are more dependent on a world market that is less open to our trade. The post-neo-colonial era has witnessed the rise of the multinational as a necessary form for the business activities of the capitalist economies; it provides the indispensable mechanism of penetration. As with earlier colonizing schemes, this one also brings with it a religious aura as cover. The following statement by Jacques G. Maisonrouge, president of the IBM World Trade Corporation, reflects the new missionarism of growth:

> It has been our constant desire to grow, and to grow by being present in every feasible market, that has led IBM to where it is today. Wanting growth has nothing to do with imperialistic motives. Rather, it is one of the conditions necessary to remain dynamic, to remain young, and to maintain a sound level of excellence. Through time, I am sure, we will have substantial changes in the structure of the company, but one thing that will remain is our desire to grow, our desire to develop the non-U.S. markets, and to be present, as much as we can, in all the countries of the world.[22]

The problem with all this is that while classical economists since the time of Adam Smith could claim that the workings of the capitalist system, through profit maximization, led inevitably to efficient allocation of resources, no such claim can be made for the present situation where administered prices aim at a "growth" based not on efficient response to market forces, but on the long-run security or profit of large companies. One can no longer assume that producers and consumers are reasonably "free" (that is, suspended in a market setting without power to manipulate and without being manipulated).

We now know full well that we have wasted enormous amounts of the world's raw materials, capital, and labor power. But, when all other rationalizations have come tumbling, there is still that one resilient cry—no one, no system, has ever had growth like we have it. With growth everything is possible or acceptable, including waste. Hell, if the pie is expanding, there's more for everyone (including the garbage collector). And it is this claim that runs like a thread through all of the business literature, corporate reports, and testimony by business executives before government committees. We grow, we know how to grow, and growth is life. Stop our global growth and, in the words of Mr. Kendall of Pepsico, "It's like killing the goose that laid the golden egg."[23]

This globalism was summed up by Robert Stevenson, executive vice-president for international operations of the Ford Motor Company:

> It is our goal to be in every single country there is, Iron Curtain countries, Russia, China. We at Ford Motor Company look at a world map without any boundaries. We don't consider ourselves basically an American company. We are a multinational company. And when we approach a government that doesn't like the U.S., we always say "Who do you like? Britain? Germany? We carry a lot of flags. We export from every country."[24]

In what meaningful sense does this hell-bent "competition" of a handful of companies (in each product area) to carve up world markets reflect efficient allocation of the world's resources? The "market" only exists in a particular country if the "host government" and one or more foreign companies decide they want it to exist. Who does the government of a country really represent? What if that government only exists because the U.S. government wants it to or has overthrown its predecessor? Does the presence of a multinational company still reflect efficient allocation of resources through the market? Even the expansion of that company into the local market will have more to do with the decisions of that host country's elite and the parent multinational than with any consumer demand. As an illustration, Pepsico, for a time, was hamstrung in its operations in Brazil and the Philippines by a nationalist political climate. But with U.S. interference, that "climate" changed and so did Pepsico's ability to operate.[25] Clearly, the actions of the U.S. government in terms of military aid, training, CIA cover activities, etc., were far more important than any market demand of local consumers.

Even if we assume neutral governments down the line and an "open" market, it would still be a highly oligopolistic one, with all of the "distortions" of advertising, administered prices, market sharing, etc. And it can be safely argued that lesser developed countries are even more vulnerable to this sort of distortion than those with more "sophisticated" markets.

Any attempt to stimulate demand in the current world situation may be wasteful, given the obvious and pressing need of the majority of people for necessities. But a multinational enters a particular market not to serve the needs of that society but rather to increase sales "by any means necessary"; therefore social priorities inevitably become distorted.

One needs to belabor this point, for if one accepts the multinationals' massive propaganda about the coming world order it almost seems as if the competitive capitalism of Adam Smith's dream is being reincarnated in this decade on a multinational scale. This global dream, for example, was offered by the vice-president of Caterpillar Tractor:

> We are a multinational company, treating foreign operators as co-equals with domestic, in both structure and policy, willing to allocate resources without regard to national frontiers.
>
> We will one day become a transnational company— a multinational business, managed and owned by people of different nationalities.[26]

This abandonment of the nation-state involves giving up a unit of government in which people have some chance of exercising control over these corporations, for a business internationalism in which there is none. These corporations hope to escape the fetters of popular control or regulation, but are unwilling to give up the protection and intervention of the world's most powerful states—the mother countries. *If a "transnational" company is meant to be one that will operate under a new international umbrella of big powers in Kissinger's new order of stability, then the corporations are having it both ways. And that, of course, is what they want.*

The multipolar world of peace which the Nixon Doctrine aimed to create is really a mechanism for asserting new rules for the game—the dominance of the rich nations over the poor; or more accurately of the rich nations' corporations over the rest of the world. For the "structure of peace" in the post-neo-colonial era will be a structure of arrangements among the powerful nations to maintain the "proper" international environment to protect the sanctity of foreign investment. It assumes a commonality of interest and a sharing of responsibility among the powerful that transcends their competitive differences.

Multinational corporations require multinational agreements on preserving stability in the world, whether the "stability" is threatened by "terrorists" in the Mideast who blow up pipelines or by democratically elected expropriators in Chile. The contradiction in all this is the expectation on the part of the multinationals and their government that, as they grow further away from the needs of the American people, and less under their control, they can enlist more of their government's support. It further assumes that the rest of the world's people will acquiesce and even assist in this scheme.

chapter 7

THE MAKING
OF AN
ENERGY
CRISIS

The Energy Crisis first surfaced as a major public issue somewhere in the midst of Mr. Nixon's Watergate troubles, and he came to cling to it as his most reliable political life preserver. Questions at press conferences about his personal financial dealings were met with responses about his heroic ploys in the Mideast to "bring us fuel this winter." There was one particularly farcical moment immediately following the firing of special Watergate prosecutor Archibald Cox when Nixon spoke to the nation, and, instead of dealing with what had been called the "October Massacre," dawdled happily on gas rationing, new nuclear power plants, Alaskan pipelines, and negotiations with the Arabs.

All of this energy-crisis talk had a favorable fallout for some. The oil companies had a weapon against environmentalists who stopped their pipelines and liberals who challenged their tax breaks. And there were those who wanted to build nuclear power plants, increase government military spending, "ensure uninterrupted access to foreign sources," or simply mess up public beaches. Indeed, the electric power companies, the oil lobby, and the advertising council were gleefully jumping all over the energy issues, telling us how much they were doing to solve the shortage, asking that they be unhampered in this work, and explaining that it was all the problem of the average person who overheated his house or drove too fast. Gas prices doubled, government controls came off, and the oil companies scored their biggest quarterly profits during the peak periods of crisis.

National chauvinism and corporate profit-making were once again united as they had been in the best days of the Cold War, and it seemed as though the general "nonrenewable-resources crisis" would provide the necessary substitute for anticommunism. This was the leitmotif of a spate of articles in the business press: "There is a big problem but it has been caused by meddling with the corporations. End that meddling and solve the problem." This was also the administration's theme. Even the response of Nixon's critics was most often divided and weak. They tended to accept the view that the foreign oil-producing countries were gouging us, and found it hard to condemn the more marginal turn-off-your-lightbulb solutions that were offered. The energy crisis was fast giving rise to another antilitter campaign.

There seemed little to stand in the way of a developing national consensus that this was one of our "interests" and that we needed a unified foreign policy to pursue it. Nixon, so discredited in other matters, seemed to have nearly unanimous support on this pursuit of "our" Mideast oil needs. Our growth, and therefore our survival, apparently depended on controlling the supply of oil.

To challenge that consensus means to go to the root of how the American economy functions. Anything less misses the point. For example, what would be the implications of zero growth for the functioning of the American economy? Would it mean zero new investment and zero expansion to new products? Would it mean growth in the public sector to replace private invention and initiative? Would it mean a planned socialist economy? Or at least a middling Swedish-type one?

One cannot curtail America's economic growth without curtailing the system itself. The production of unwanted junk, the catering to misplaced consumer emotions, planned obsolescence, indeed, the raising of consumerism and materialism to near religious frenzy, all of this is waste and all of this is central to the system's workings. It is this reality which makes a hash of the best intentions of the environmentalists. It reduces them to so many naive handwringers in the minds of many, and sets them up as grist for a business press eager to picture them as meddlers in the soundly run affairs of pragmatic corporate officials.

The environmentalists are certainly well intentioned, but there has been something essentially apolitical about their approach. Apolitical not in the sense of being unwilling to lobby congressmen (that's their meat) but rather in their unwillingness to connect social issue to political and economic structure. For example, David Brower, former director of the Sierra Club, often shocks audiences with the statistic that the two hundred million people in the U.S. expend more energy on air-conditioning than the eight hundred million people of China do on all of their energy needs. Which, on one level, shows that we are rich and wasteful and that they are poor and thrifty. But the fact is that if we had to make do with the amount of energy available to the Chinese we would have chaos and starvation. And not simply because we are personally wasteful. We do not have a social structure that permits energy to be used frugally and socially. Neither feudal China nor the socialist one that has replaced it have been *in the main* committed to consumerism and private consumption as a way of life. Allocation of resources is a question of social system, not individual habit of mind.

Nor should criticism of the corporations focus on "waste"—at least not the marginal waste of unrecycled cans. It is rather what is *in* the cans that tends to be wasteful. It is the most rational workings of the corporations which are the problem, not the fringe. To focus on the oil spill is to miss the waste of the oil that is not spilled. The question is what to do about the main and not the margin of the practice. During all the talk of the energy crisis it was blithely stated that within the next twelve years, the U.S. would use more energy than had been used by all of the world's people up till now. In the past thirty years the U.S. used up more of the world's nonrenewable resources than had been used throughout the rest of human history.[1] So we've gone from thirty years to twelve in this measurement of consumption, which gets us to two basic points.

First, the "world resource problem" is not caused by the world, since most of the world's people don't share in its consumption. It is caused most of all by the American economy which consumes between 30 and 60 percent of any given resource.[2] Indeed, not only does the American economy consume about four times more energy than Japan, and two and a half times more than West Germany; if we include Western Europe as a whole, the developed capitalist governments are now consuming over 80 percent of all resources being produced by the world's population of several billion.[3]

Second, this is being picked up on now, not because the problem has just begun, but because for the first time the U.S. is dependent upon external resource supplies. As *Fortune* observed: "American industry has been turning increasingly to foreign sources. A net exporter of raw materials until World War II, the U.S. has been an importer ever since."[4]

We are only visibly experiencing the problem now, but it began long ago and the U.S. corporations were the central factor in its creation. The fact that much of these resources formerly came from within our borders does not ease the problem. The U.S. was one of the last great reservoirs of world resources—a virgin treasure—and it was simply abused.

We have had ample domestic oil supplies and have wasted them. But in addition to wasting what we found within our borders, our corporations have largely determined the rate of exploitation of foreign sources. And it has been our government which maintained the power of those corporations to do just that. This has been illustrated throughout the history of the exploitation of Persian Gulf oil.

In the crucial Middle Eastern fields, oil was first discovered in Iran in 1913. It was Winston Churchill

himself who quickly recognized its military importance. Ships powered by oil could go farther and
carry more than those running on coal. Oil soon
became the premium energy source in industry as
well as transportation. At first it was English and
French corporations which dominated the exploration, refining, and retailing of Middle Eastern oil.
But in the 1930s, the big five U.S. corporations*
moved into Saudi Arabia as part of the Arabian-
American Oil Company (ARAMCO) consortium.
After the Second World War the U.S. was able to
quickly increase its control to 42 percent of the estimated oil reserves in the Middle East.[5] Moves by the
locals to challenge that power were simply smashed.

The most startling challenge to the foreign companies occurred in the early fifties when a noncommunist prime minister of Iran, Mohammed Mossadegh, attempted to nationalize Iranian oil. There was
widespread popular support for this move within
Iran. This was natural enough as the country was
horribly poor and its major asset was spilling out
to the world economy with no apparent advantage to
most of its people. While Mossadegh had no desire to
deny that oil to the West, he wanted to see that the
Iranians got a decent price for it. This would have
had two effects. First, it would have provided capital
for development (including oil technology), and second, it would have kept some of that oil in the ground

---

* Standard of New Jersey (Exxon), Mobil, Gulf, Standard of California, and Texaco—these together with BP and Shell make up the
big seven oil companies.

a bit longer. But the capitalist countries were on what *Fortune* called "an energy joy ride."[6] "Cheap" energy meant that the locals got a ridiculously low price at the barrelhead, the corporations got huge profits between the wellhead and the consumer's gas-tank, and the oil got pumped out at a faster and cheaper rate than was good, in the long run, for any-body except the corporate executives and top stock-holders.

When Mossadegh, in his innocence, attempted to change all that, this eminently bourgeois, democratic gentleman, educated in the best Western tradition, found himself up against an array of capitalist corpo-rate power that even Vladimir Lenin would have underestimated. The major oil companies got to-gether and with great show of unity and economic power stood behind the British oil companies in Iran to force Mossadegh to "drink his oil." Mossadegh and the Iranian people tried holding out until finally the American CIA, in one of their more well-documented escapades, stepped in to administer the *coup de grace.*[7] Mossadegh was overthrown and the Shah, an obvi-ously totalitarian monarch, was installed to protect the interests of the free world. The Mossadegh ex-ample kept other Persian Gulf countries away from nationalizations and firmly under Western domi-nance until 1970. One side effect of the Iranian coup was that the U.S. companies obtained 40 percent of the oil action in Iran, where before it had been an exclusively British deal.[8]

The coming apart of the American oil position

overseas in the sixties occurred for the same reasons the U.S. failed in Cuba and Vietnam: overextension and excessive greed by the U.S., competition from increasingly strong capitalist nations, and the growing resistance of Third World countries.

The break began in 1960 when five oil-producing countries formed the Organization of Petroleum Exporting Countries (OPEC) and moved toward collective bargaining with the big seven oil companies. This was an unheard-of step and oil company executives quickly professed that it would fail—the oil countries would once again be divided and conquered.

And, on the basis of past experience, this is what should have happened. There had been much talk in the fifties about greater producer participation, particularly in the Arab world where rising nationalism was a new factor. Different plans were worked out ostensibly to accomplish this, but the opposite somehow always occurred. The net income of the oil companies, as a percentage of net assets, *actually rose* from 61 percent in 1948–49 to 72 percent in 1958–60.[9] The Arabs were given more, but not at the expense of the big seven oil companies. The Arab sheiks and other monarchs increased their income impressively from 78 percent of net assets in 1948–49 to 130 percent for 1958–60.[10] While that meant more dollars to cover their luxuries, military expenditures, and foreign savings, it was done at the expense of an incredible waste of their countries' resources—a fivefold rise in production.

If we think of an energy crisis in terms of the over-rapid consumption of a limited amount of fossil fuel, and particularly a limited amount of oil, the most versatile and useful of such fuels, then pumping out five times more oil from the ground will undoubtedly contribute to long-run depletion. Rationally then, a decision to multiply production should be made in terms of most effectively utilizing limited resources over a long future timeframe to meet the needs of the world population. But in this case it was not the world's people, or even the American and Mideast peoples, who were making those decisions. It was seven multinational corporations, operating through local leaders whom they had helped select and maintain in power, and all done with the necessary military and political backing of the U.S. government. The U.S. government gave tax breaks on the Saudi operation to Standard Oil of New Jersey and to Mobil, and trained the Saudi army and air force through military assistance as well. When Ibn Saud, who ruled Saudi Arabia by-the-grace-of-Allah, became a nuisance in 1966, it was the U.S. who backed his successor King Faisal (who also ruled by-the-grace-of-Allah). The grace of Allah, unless combined with the grace of the U.S., was no longer sufficient for rule in the Mideast.

In this period the alliances between the most primitively reactionary of Arab rulers and the U.S. corporations seemed permanent. The seven oil companies had an unquestioned monopoly over production and retailing, the Arab monarchs restrained their appetites for wealth, and the power of the U.S. government and its British ally to back all this up ("to enforce the terms of understanding") was supreme.

As reported by Joe Stork of the Middle East Research and Information Project (MERIP),* those were the "bonanza years." Between 1948 and 1960 Mideastern oil brought in 28.4 billion dollars in receipts. As a measure of just how good a business it was, operating costs accounted for only $4.8 billion, and a paltry $1.3 billion of that $28.4 billion had to be reinvested in fixed assets related to production. The rest was gravy to be divided between the local governments and the oil companies. The locals got $9.4 billion, which was pretty good, given that they didn't have to share it with the local citizenry, but not as good as the $12.8 billion profits which the oil companies sent back to their home offices.[11]

These enormous profits created what Marx called a contradiction of capitalism. It was so attractive a profit picture that other smaller or independent companies in the U.S., as well as state-controlled and private companies abroad, were bursting to jump in. It should be added that during this period in which the U.S. oil companies controlled about 42 percent of Mideast reserves,[12] they were not sending that oil to U.S. markets but rather exclusively to Europe, Japan, and the Third World. It was the time of their

---

* MERIP is a research collective which publishes a monthly report that is concerned with the political economy of the Middle East. They can be contacted at P.O. Box 48; Cambridge, Mass., 02138 or P.O. Box 3122; Columbia Heights Station; Washington, D.C., 20010.

time for these multinationals; U.S.-based with the backing of American military power, extracting oil in Saudi Arabia to sell at U.S.-owned gas stations abroad. Never has the concept of "national interest" been more simply and clearly connected with profit-making. One could not even have argued that the Arabian oil was vital for our domestic needs, since the oil for U.S. consumption was still coming primarily from Texas, Louisiana, and California. It was not until the 1970s when we had come to import 7 percent of our oil from the Mideast and anticipate a need for 50 percent by 1980, that the national interest in oil for the first time began to transcend the profit-making interests of those five companies and related, necessarily, to the survival of the whole system. Corporate America needed an ever-expanding supply of oil even more than the profits. It was no longer prudent to let the boards of directors of oil companies have exclusive say over Mideast or energy policy.

It should be added that the other capitalist governments were not about to go along with U.S. policy in the Mideast in quite the same fashion as they had in Vietnam. Their interests in the oil fields were far more crucial than they had been in the rice paddies. The increasing economic and military strength of the Common Market nations and Japan gave them a growing industrial incentive to ensure their access to oil, as well as the wherewithal to stand up to the U.S. The Marshall Plan had sown the seeds of its own discontent.

The previous decade from 1960 to 1970 had been a transitional one. European governments were becoming concerned about U.S. predominance over their supplies (remember French editor Servan-Schreiber's famous attack, *The American Challenge*) at the same time that they were also getting stronger. In the late fifties some mavericks like Italy's state-owned ENI (Ente Nazionale Idrocarburi) tried to undermine the majors with some limited success. But with the formation of OPEC in the sixties, competition became respectable and institutionalized.

The U.S. government and the big oil companies were alarmed, but the U.S. military (including the CIA) was pinned down elsewhere and suffering opposition for the first time. The debacle of the Bay of Pigs and Kennedy's public repudiation of the CIA had made it much more difficult to have Mossadegh-type operations. It became even more difficult after the nightmare of the CIA's overthrow of Diem in Vietnam, which resulted in the entry of massive numbers of American troops. The forces of what Nixon called "isolationism" (and others might term sanity) were rising in the U.S. Few had any stomach left for the kind of foreign adventure that begins with a few "advisers" and ends with a half-million Americans bogged down in some jungle or desert.

The Arab leaders, just like those in Venezuela and Indonesia, were having their own troubles and were less inclined to collaborate with the U.S. They were under increasing pressure from nationalist forces that derided the sellout of their nation's resources.

At the same time, they were stimulated by the examples of the Cubans and Vietnamese. In Venezuela students looked to Castro as a model of independence from U.S. corporations and put pressure on Betancourt to do the same. Rulers like Betancourt hardly needed the urging, for they were aware that unless they assumed some portion of the mantle of progress, they too would go the way of the Batistas and the Ngo Dinh Diems.

In the Mideast the ever-present specter of Arab nationalism, led by Gamal Nasser, spread far beyond the borders of Egypt, and there were few young Arabs who could get to a radio set or who studied abroad who were not touched by his anticolonialist precepts.

Nasser, who, in the mid-fifties, had nationalized the Suez Canal over the military opposition of the French, English, and Israeli armies, upped the ante in the sixties—thundering primarily against the "neo-colonialism" of the U.S. as the worst menace in the Mideast. This neo-colonialist presence was identified with the oil companies' exploitation of Arab resources, helped along by Arab rulers whose governments and armies were run for them by U.S. advisers. Even decadent old Ibn Saud, who went to live in Cairo after he was deposed as the leader of Saudi Arabia, warmed to Nasser's message.

There was a swelling perception that the resources of the Mideast belonged to all of the Arab and Iranian people, that some puppets had sold out these resources, and that the people should reclaim them from the puppets and their U.S. and British backers. There was an added element, particularly stressed by Nasser, that the Arabs and Persians were Third World peoples whose interests coincided with other Third World peoples. The struggles of the Vietnamese and Algerians were very widely reported in the Mideast and were often cited as proof of the fact that the foreigners could be successfully taken on.

The British were the first casualty of this shift in perception. Guerilla movements developed in Yemen and particularly around the city of Aden, Britain's main naval base. By the end of the sixties, the British had to pull out of their Mideast strongholds, retaining only advisory functions in the Persian Gulf sheikdoms.

This time the U.S. was unable to simply move in to replace the old colonial apparatus; neither the American nor Arab people would have tolerated it. Western rule had to be asserted in what Nixon has called "more subtle ways." And it also had to be asserted at a time when the Western powers themselves were more and more divided, and when the U.S. was bogged down in the disaster of Vietnam.

The oil monarchs began to grow uneasy under all this pressure and to smell some new opportunities for their own survival. Then, too, the socialist states of Algeria and Iraq contained oil, and they began to show some leadership in wringing concessions from the companies.

In 1958, Kassem, who rivaled Nasser's leadership

of Arab socialism, had come to power in Iraq. He attempted to exceed Nasser's anti-imperialist rhetoric and was in a vital spot to do it, given that Iraq was a major oil producer. He took Iraq out of the U.S.-inspired Baghdad pact, and developed an economic and technical aid agreement with the Soviet Union. The Soviets by then were developed enough to deliver such aid. As another sign of changing times, Kassem moved to open a 6o percent portion of the oil concession (then exclusively British run) to independent companies for development.[13] All of this was incredibly threatening, but the Western response of isolating Iraq from the other oil producers was still an effective gambit. Production, and therefore revenues, in Iraq were held down, while they were dramatically increased in neighboring Kuwait, Iran, and Saudi Arabia. The oil companies also fostered national differences with Iraq's neighbors as well as doing whatever they could to stir opposition to Kassem's rule within Iraq. The CIA was particularly active in this period. Kassem was killed in a coup and the new Baathist regime was more conciliatory.

But the following years of shifts in the Iraqi government and fitful attempts to develop a new arrangement failed. The result was a most disastrous development for the oil companies—the Iraq-Soviet agreement of June 1969. The U.S. had lost the Cold War —at least in Iraq. Iraq had suffered through the sixties when the oil companies' plan to keep oil production down had denied the Iraqi economy much needed capital. But the political lessons had been clear, and Iraq entered the seventies in a very strong position to deal against the companies.

In Iran the U.S. had been more fortunate, at least on the surface. Following the CIA's installation of the Shah after the deposition of Mossadegh, massive military aid and training seemed to ensure a period of stable U.S. influence. The Shah was indebted to the U.S. not only for past services but future survival. But this stability soon proved tenuous. Iran has a relatively large population of over thirty million, and the ratio of oil revenue per capita is very much lower than in Kuwait or Saudi Arabia. The Shah's administrative costs in controlling the population involved an inflated military payroll and a vast secret police. Together with the largesse of his royal family these costs had bankrupted him by the end of the fifties. The forces of revolution were stirring in Iran, as they were throughout the Middle East, and they had a strong anti-imperialist (read anti-U.S.) bent to them.

The Shah's response, at the prodding of his American advisers, was aimed at co-opting the discontent with a much-publicized "White Revolution" as an alternative to the Red Revolution that was becoming increasingly attractive to his people. The difference between a Red Revolution and those of another hue —be it green, white, or any other color, is that Red Revolutions aim at breaking the power of foreign corporations and overturning the power of the local ruling elites which serve them. The essence of the

White Revolution in Iran, as with similar ventures throughout the Third World, was to create the appearance of economic progress with commodity imports for a privileged class as opposed to basic industrial development. Iran's White Revolution jumped commodity imports from 485.6 million dollars in 1963–64 to just double that ($967 million in 1966–67). These were paid for by increasing oil revenues which came from increased production, or, once again, waste of the Iranian and world people's nonrenewable resources.[14]

For all the talk of revolution, and despite Iran's vastly increased oil revenues in 1973–74, *The New York Times* could report as late as June 3, 1974 that:

> Iran, where civilization flourished while Europe was barbarian, is today a country that cannot feed itself.
>
> The ruler, Shah Mohammed Riza Pahlevi, promises greatness, but 70 percent of the people are illiterate and 60 percent live at subsistence levels. Hundreds of villages are without doctors although oil revenues are flowing into the national treasury.[15]

The report also quoted the Shah as still very much concerned about the ultimate depletion of oil (estimated at thirty to sixty years) and saying that he felt pressured to do something about development.

By the end of the sixties, as the pressure mounted on local rulers like the Shah, the foreign companies began to run scared. The failure of their economic development programs had become increasingly obvious to the people under the rule of the Mideastern monarchs. The panacea was to pump in more money without changing the economic structure. But this money could only come from increased oil revenues. Profits had been maintained in the face of declining rates per barrel and an overall falling rate of profit in relation to investment. But, even aside from the rate of profit, the oil companies were uneasy. If the sixties had been troublesome, the seventies looked much worse. OPEC was stronger, anti-imperialist sentiment was rising, and rival capitalist countries were increasingly eager to step in. In addition, the Soviets had taken over the Ramalah field in Iraq.

The British were pulling out of the Persian Gulf area, and the U.S. public was hostile to foreign adventure. A new mood had to be engendered in American public opinion which would support a new U.S. "initiative" in the Mideast. The oil companies began to diversify their holdings throughout the general energy field, and, at the same time, beat the drums of an impending energy crisis which would give them the political flexibility to get away with a whole new series of scams from the Alaska ripoff to atomic breeders to a new U.S. government alliance with the Arab governments. Their alarm had caused them to come up with a new package, and, as the crisis of the seventies began to break, they were ready to turn adversity to advantage. Mideast political turmoil would produce domestic political good.

The first big crack in the current Middle Eastern situation was caused by a political coup in Libya which brought a young Moslem army officer to power.

He attempted to assume Nasser's mantle as the leader of Arab nationalism. But Colonel Qaddafi was an hysterical anticommunist, hostile to the Soviets and not at all interested in denying the West oil. As with Mossadegh, he wanted more control of his country. He proceeded to up the price and threaten nationalization. Mideast watchers sipped their coffee in the cafes of Beirut speculating about the precise moment when the U.S. axe would fall on Qaddafi as it had on Mossadegh. But it didn't.

The times were different. To begin with, the oil companies and governments could no longer present the united front of the past decades. There had been rapid growth in Japanese and Western European economies accompanied by voracious oil appetites. These other capitalist countries could not afford the political risk of following the lead of the U.S. They would refine Libya's oil and market it—*avec plaisir.*

There was also the fact that the locals had gotten together. OPEC, despite all predictions to the contrary, held its ground. So when Libya made its move and won, the other oil-producing countries quickly followed its example—even our King Faisal, even our Shah. The first concessions by the companies to the oil producers were not terribly big, but they set a precedent. Indeed, it was the first increase in the posted price of Mideast oil since 1960.

This is truly fantastic when one considers the five-fold increase in oil consumption during the 1960s. Whatever happened to supply and demand or any of the other vaunted laws of capitalist economic activity? They didn't pertain in the Mideast because competition did not exist in any real sense. When it did begin to assert itself, the oil companies, the U.S. government, and most of the American press treated it as the darkest of communist and/or Islamic plots. The laws of capitalist competition had lain dormant during the decades of monopolistic control by the oil companies, and, when they began to reappear, the corporate execs registered the kind of outraged shocks that the moneylenders did when Jesus threw them out of the temple.

Events moved very rapidly in the early seventies. Not only did the price of oil go up at the wellhead, but an effective boycott was maintained after the October War, this time by the oil-producing countries rather than the corporations.

With typical Western arrogance, the attempt of oil producers to get more control and a fair price for their oil was termed an energy crisis. Fifty years of rampant ripoff by the oil companies had been thought of as normal, indeed, a sound business environment.

The response of the oil producers did not represent a revolution. For that to happen oil revenues would have to flow into the hands of the tens of millions of Mideastern people who still live in abject poverty. But we should not underestimate what occurred. Pushed by their own people, sensing the growing weakness of the U.S., and faced with their own ballooning import costs, even reactionary rulers will move. Like Nixon, the Shah of Iran was moved by events beyond his control, and began to play his options. Although a fervent anticommunist, he sent his sister to visit Peking, established diplomatic relations with China and entered into oil and natural gas exploitation arrangements with the Soviet Union.

This served as a show of independence and a way of upping the ante, but none of it challenged the basic dependence of the Persian Gulf monarchs on the U.S. The U.S. still supplies them with military advisers and arms, their officers are still trained in Fort Leavenworth, Kansas, and much of their wealth is still invested through the New York Stock Exchange and U.S.-owned banks.

Indeed, the much-publicized Yamani Plan, named after Saudi Arabia's energetic minister of petroleum, offers all of Saudi Arabia's future oil production to the United States in return for the right to buy into the American oil interests in Saudi Arabia. It is the opposite of nationalization—it is co-option.

But such arrangements are intrinsically unstable, for the rulers who make them are anachronisms. There are strong pressures throughout the Third World and certainly the Arab world for modernization and economic development. The price of that development, whether it be a socialist plan or a "progressive Moslem one," is greater control over the world-wide marketing and general exploitation of a people's resources.

In the case of oil, what this means is not simply haggling about the posted well prices or percentage ownership of the small part of a company that is bringing the oil up from the ground. It means control over all phases—the vertical integration of drilling, refining, and marketing. We will know when that has happened not by studying posted barrel figures or OPEC resolutions but by the very visible appearance of Algerian, Saudi, and Iranian gas stations in Salinas, California, or Rochester, New York, competing with each other to sell us their oil. While this would bring lower gas prices to the consumers in the U.S., it would play havoc with oil company profits.

This, of course, was not close to happening in the early seventies for all the hysterical energy-crisis talk, nor was the threat of a serious and sustained cutoff of Arab supplies foreseen. Perhaps the most authoritative U.S. government statement was made by James E. Akins, the State Department's top energy man. He discounted such possibilities, and stated that all the talk of Arab participation in the oil companies was actually aiming at locking the Arabs ever more closely into supplying the Western consumer.[16] What was at issue was the old-fashioned question "How much does it cost?" And the assumption of the American media has been that the price being asked was outlandish, blackmail, etc.

Newsweek magazine, during the energy crisis, had a cover of the typical Arab in costume (the model it later turned out was Jewish and from New York) standing by a gas pump cutting off the flow. It would have been perhaps more accurate to have shown an Arab with his finger in a dike around a sea of Persian Gulf oil, vainly attempting to prevent its rushing through. As Akins wrote, summarizing the crisis:

"Much more important [than increased revenues], indeed of overwhelming importance to the changing world oil picture, was that the OPEC countries, for the first time, began to recognize and discuss openly the fact that their reserves were exhaustible and should be conserved."[17]

Even the most greedy and reactionary of the monarchs had come to see that the indiscriminate pumping of their oil, in the absence of commensurate and profound economic development, would leave them in possession of a kingdom of sand in a matter of decades. Nor was this an unrealistic fear, as Akins affirms:

> Kuwait recently stopped expansion and plans to keep production at three million barrels per day. At this level, Kuwait will have oil for a couple of generations—but even this is a short period for a nation; and Kuwait's prospects of finding more oil are very small. Iran has stated that it will limit production to eight million barrels per day before the end of this decade; production will be held there for eight or ten years and then will decline. . . . North Africa's reserves are not large enough to play a dominant role in world oil in 1980.[18]

He goes on to say that, should Saudi Arabia accede to rampant maximum production, it "would also ruin itself in the process . . . even its enormous reserves would soon be exhausted."[19]

In this context, the conflict is not merely between the host countries and the oil companies, but rather between the producing countries and those who would consume their oil. In a sense, the oil companies, once the dominant personae of Mideast oil politics, have been pushed to the side of the stage, and the consumers, particularly the capitalist governments, can no longer be guided simply by corporate needs, but, rather, by the survival of their entire economies.

The position of the United States was one of calling for the advanced capitalist consumers of oil to maintain a common bargaining position in order to hold down the price. Akins spoke for the U.S. in stating this position:

> If consumers encourage companies to resist further price increases, this should also cause no surprise. Many consumers already believe that the companies have not been adequately vigorous in resisting producer demand as they could and usually did pass on to the consumer any tax increases. The producer governments have banded together in a well functioning organization. Their immediate adversaries are only the companies—an unequal contest.[20]

It should be understood here that by "consumers" is meant not the world's households but rather the five or six major industrial countries in the world. The program, then, is one of bringing the power of the governments even more clearly to bear behind the companies and against the producers. The united front of the capitalist governments was supposed to back up the united front of the major oil companies which was now falling apart. But at last report, the other governments were altogether too nervous about their own supplies

and were busily working out their separate deals. But
the real difficulty with all this is that it avoids the
source of the problem—waste by a relative few.

The increase in world consumption of oil in the
next decade doesn't anticipate a major rise in consumption by "have-not" nations. Indeed Akins points
out they are more and more being excluded as consumers because of rising prices. On the first price rise
"India was unable to absorb the increase and was
forced to cut back petroleum purchases proportionately."[21] The fact is "the underdeveloped consuming
countries . . . had counted on declining real fuel
prices to sustain their economic growth."[22]

And the fact is that most of the increased drain
on Mideastern oil, or indeed all oil outside the U.S.,
is by the U.S., which by 1980 will be consuming
twenty-five million barrels of oil per day, half of that
derived from sources outside of the United States.[23]
If this does not happen, then the world crisis will
seem a good deal less severe. But it will happen if the
American economic system goes its merry way. It is
amazing that even as perceptive an observer as Akins
ends his analysis with a wistful reference to conserving energy and working toward some crash shift to
nuclear energy by the turn of the century. His other
hope is an urgent investment program in extraction
from shale, heavy oil, or tar sands, but he notes
gloomily that these methods "all require capital investments on the scale of $5–$7 billion for each
million barrels per day of capacity."[24] As with so

many other schemes for energy substitutes, that means developing a noncompetitive source of fuel beyond the reach of Third World countries.

These alternatives will not work in this century, and the actual scenario will be one of an intensified scramble for oil (along with most other nonrenewable resources) that will leave those countries lacking economic power out in the cold, and sow the seeds of conflict for those who possess it.

That it need not be this way is obvious. What we do need, instead of multinational corporations backed by the might or "consumer solidarity" of the big capitalist powers, is a notion of social planning and development which would nurture, rather than squander, scarce resources. Even our own regulated public utilities provide some very limited precedents for such planning. But this was not the drift of energy-crisis talk. Both the corporations and the U.S. government were pursuing the same goal of scaring the American public into acceptance of even greater corporate discretion and power, rather than less. *If we had dealt with the real energy crisis presented by the waste of resources, rather than on the manufactured one of deliberate interruptions of supplies, then a different set of solutions might have seemed likely.*

The energy crisis was a PR campaign, carefully orchestrated through totally unnecessary disruptions of the flow of fuel and gas, as well as completely arbitrary increases in their prices. It aimed at showing us not that the energy companies had wasted resources, but rather that they had been fettered in their attempt to harness and discover them, and that if only they were unfettered all would be well.

We are witnessing increasing corporate and governmental power drives in the energy field—not to make the corporations more responsible to the Mideastern or American people, but to give them a stronger bargaining position. (Indeed, a senate subcommittee recently revealed that State Department oil expert Akins—later ambassador to Saudi Arabia—had participated in the collusion of the oil companies in their foreign negotiations.)[25]

Mideast expert Joe Stork sums up his excellent study of the energy crisis by saying: "No one disputes that the resources, including the energy resources, are there for the future if they are used wisely and well. Who is to control them, and who is to profit from that control, will be the focus of struggle in all countries and regions in the coming decade."[26]

Before the intrusion of the Arab oil boycott, the scenario for the seventies was one of growth and more growth for the waste economies, dwarfing all that had come before. Growth rates from 1970 through 1973 chalked up an astounding 7 percent per annum in constant dollars. The World Bank predicted that the combined GNP of the developed countries would rise from $2,000 billion in 1970 to $3,000 billion in 1980, at constant prices. The per capita income in those countries was expected to rise from $2,400 in 1970 to $3,600 by 1980.[27] This quarter of the world population would receive 80 percent of the increase in the world's income during the seventies, thereby heightening the inequality between them and the three quarters of the world that is "developing."[28] As for the latter, their per capita income would rise from $180 to just under $280 if all of the development targets were kept, including the pledge of the developed countries to commit .7 percent of their GNP to development.[29] But even this meager goal was not being met, and the developed countries, despite their booming economies, were projecting a lower aid commitment. In the case of the U.S. it was to drop from a miserable .31 percent of GNP in 1970 to .24 percent in 1975.[30] (Thus, the U.S. was willing to commit a smaller amount for long-term, low-interest development loans through the World Bank system—including the International Monetary Fund—than the pet food industry spends on advertising.)

The energy crisis forced an awareness of the vulnerability of advanced economies to the Third World in much the same way that guerrilla warfare, as practiced by the Chinese and Vietnamese, forced a breakthrough of awareness on the military and political fronts. It was soon perceived in the developed countries that oil was not the only resource found in Third World countries which was vital to their production, and which might be denied or become more costly.

In one example of such awakening, H. J. Maidenberg writing in *The New York Times* business section noted:

> The industrial nations, which have grown fat largely on huge servings of cheap raw materials such as foodstuffs, fibers, minerals and fuel, are facing an increasingly costly diet.

> Whether the costlier rations are the result of a managed crisis like the petroleum embargo, or reflect speculative factors in world commodity markets, is of little comfort to the non-communist nations.

> The question facing those nations is whether their problem of commodity price inflation is a temporary condition or whether it presages a historic economic change in relationships between the industrial powers and the poor lands that have traditionally been suppliers of raw materials.

> What is clear is that an unprecedented peacetime rise in the price of all basic commodities is overwhelming such industrial powers as Japan and those in Western Europe.[31]

For the first time in the postwar decade, the industrial nations had to consider the "cost" of such raw materials, a cost which should, by any reckoning of economic efficiency, have been taken into consideration all along. The fact that Third World resources had been historically "cheap" was a result of the relative economic and military weakness of those undeveloped countries, which put them at the mercy of the world powers. With the changed political situation of the seventies, and particularly the disunity of the Western powers and the declining power of the U.S., Third World options were increasing.

It was not a matter of "blackmail" but rather a redress of grievances—the Third World had been getting less than it should have for its raw materials, compared to what the developed countries (in particular Japan and Western Europe) were getting for the manufactured goods they had been able to produce as a result of the importation of those materials. As the Chairman of Barclays Bank International, Anthony F. Tuke, stated:

> People living in the richer countries must admit, in all honesty, that the current increase in commodity prices is well overdue. The rise in the price of manufactured goods, has, until recently, exceeded the increase in commodity prices. . . . Let us remind ourselves that over two-thirds of the money that industrial countries pay out for raw materials usually finds its way back in terms of orders for our manufactured goods.[32]

With the exception of a few particularly endowed and less populated countries, most prominently the oil producers, it did not seem likely that increased raw material prices would do much to close the gap between the have-not countries and the industrial ones. Most of these prices are not as easily controlled at the sources of production, nor as critical as oil, making OPEC-type arrangements less likely. On the other hand, Third World countries must buy manufactured goods from large Western oligopolistic corporations. As these corporations are not victims of free markets they can easily pass on the increased price of raw materials to the consumer. The simultaneous gasoline price rises and increased profits of the multinational oil companies were a startling example of this. Most Third World countries found their development plans in shambles as a result of increased oil prices in the energy crisis. In addition, many Third World countries are raw material importers. In particular, the miracle export economies like South Korea were hurt even more than Japan by rising prices, since their economies were more tightly locked into a few key imports.

In the final analysis, it did not seem likely that the relatively "free market" of raw material commodity production would come out on top, as compared to industrial goods prices; nor that it would be a source of serious development funds for most of the Third World. As the First National City Bank's economic letter pointed out in January of 1974: "City Bank's view is that the present high prices will encourage producers to raise more foodstuffs, dig out more minerals, and pump more oil, thus causing the chronic surpluses that have traditionally caused downturns in commodity prices."[33]

What it all meant was that the industrial countries hold the main cards. Whatever the temporary shifts of a given year, economic power depends generally on capital investment and industrialization, and the Third World was still way behind. Indeed, they had fallen further behind in the period since the Second World War. Their eagerness to seize upon this moment of economic uncertainty for some immediate gain was a reflection of their overall desperation.

The commodities crisis sent the large corporations scrambling for new sources of materials which would, in the long run, ensure their power over the markets for finished industrial goods. In the process, there was some competitive fallout favorable to some of the poorer nations as a result of the rivalry between these corporations and the governments behind them. However, the main effect was that the powerful were able to spread their tentacles further, just as the oil companies using tax-free dollars were able to buy up new leases on oil-rich land. Aside from the few oil monarchs, the rest of the Third World possessed no real countervailing power against these corporations. They were, in fact, competing among themselves for foreign investment, which was increasingly the only source of much needed and ever scarce capital for their development. At the price of obtaining this capital, they surrendered even more of their sovereignty at the moment they most desired to retain it.

The one positive effect of all this was a recognition in the advanced world that a crisis existed in relations with the Third World. Until the energy crisis, few in the West had felt a need to acknowledge it.

chapter 8

MYTH
OF A
SHRINKING
WORLD

In the quarter of a century following World War II there developed a generalized assumption in the rich countries that the problems of the poor countries were gradually being solved. That this assumption had no foundation in fact did not mitigate its usefulness. It enabled citizens of the economies of waste to acquiesce to the ripoffs of the multinational corporations. There was always the convenient rationalization that if the lot of the poor countries wasn't improving, it was hardly our fault, since we had tried through a myriad of much-publicized programs like Point Four, Food For Peace, Care, and the Peace Corps to share our riches. If Third World countries were not close to our levels of consumption by now, it was due to their lack of industriousness or perhaps their preference for a simpler life.

In the past the U.S. Department of State has been a major source for the optimistic view of Third World development, but even its recent surveys are gloomy. In former Secretary of State Rogers' 1972 report to Congress, he stated that in the LDCs (meaning lesser developed countries—a euphemism for have-nots) "there are more children not in school today than there were ten years ago." There has been a good deal of investment in school systems as a high-priority item, but it has not kept abreast with population increases. According to this same report, "Up to 1.5 billion people in the LDC's remain hungry" and "Young workers flood the job markets creating mass unemployment and underemployment. The rates of unemployment and underemployment range up to

more than 30 percent in many developing countries
(higher than the United States experienced in the
worst years of the depression in the 1930's)."[1]

Rogers' survey of what was once vaunted to be a
quarter of a century of progress concluded that:

> It is now clear that present efforts to help the less
> developed world cannot reduce the gap between rich
> and poor nations. But we must seek at least to help
> them achieve a more equitable sharing in the progress
> occurring in the developing world, giving special at-
> tention to the poorest countries.[2]

This shift, from the goal of full and meaningful
employment of the world's people to a program of
welfare to control the level of discontent, assumes a
permanent depression in LDCs relative to the waste
economies. We must give them enough of a handout
(flow of resources) so that they will stay within our
sphere of influence and not develop revolutions which
might deny us access to them. Again the Secretary of
State (before the energy crisis):

> The United States has a clear interest in facilitating
> the flow of resources to the developing world. We
> are increasingly linked to the developing countries
> in international trade and investment. U.S. imports
> of energy fuels and minerals are expected to increase
> from $8 billion in 1970 to more than $31 billion by
> 1985. The known reserves of many minerals are
> located in the developing countries. Chile, Peru,
> Zambia, and Zaire supply most of the world's export-
> able copper. Malaysia, Bolivia, and Thailand account
> for 70 percent of the tin in international trade. By
> 1985 we may be importing half or more of our petro-

leum from a dozen developing countries. The LDC's
are also becoming increasingly important markets for
U.S. exports. In 1970, 30 percent of all U.S. exports
went to the developing countries. U.S. corporations
have invested some $30 billion in the developing
countries, and these investments are growing at about
10 percent a year.[3]

That sets the stage about as clearly as any campus
radical rhetorician would want. This assessment
leaves out only the punchline: that increased frustra-
tion in the Third World over American-inspired
development programs has led to greater resistance
to the surrender of their resources to American
corporations. America needs more and more of these
strategic resources from a world that is more and
more skeptical about giving them up on the old
terms. The conflict over Middle East oil is only a
more visible manifestation of this tension. Secretary
Rogers mentioned our relationship with Chile. And
it was not long after this report that the Allende government was overthrown, due in large part to a consistent U.S. government policy of strangling the Chilean economy through adroit manipulation of aid
and loan schemes that had been set up ostensibly to
help the LDCs.

The real purposes of American economic and military programs must be judged by the concrete results
they produced and not by the claims made for them
at UNESCO meetings. Those results were once again
summarized most accurately in reference to the preservation of economic elites by Secretary Rogers:

Perhaps even more troublesome than the contrasts among developing countries is the inequity in income distribution within countries where half the population generally receive no more than 5–20 percent of the income. During the 1950's and 1960's, it was hoped that high levels of investment, made possible in part by foreign aid, would foster sufficient economic growth to insure that all levels of society would benefit. In this way problems of employment and income distribution would be minimized, as they were in Western Europe and the United States during their periods of industrialization. By the end of the 1960's it was apparent that a similar pattern has not emerged in the LDC's, and that in many countries the position of people at the lower end of the income scales had become worse despite over-all growth.[4]

This last sentence is an incredible judgment of the Cold War decades in which the U.S. virtually insisted that the Third World follow its prefabricated model for development. It was a model that contained the basics of our system—a "free" market, private ownership of most of the economy, limited government planning, and the creation of business elites to run the whole show. Indeed, it was a model rammed down peoples' throats behind the whole Red scare of the free-world mythology. Not to follow this model meant being soft on the key issues of freedom and communism. It reached ludicrous heights at times, as when Ngo Dinh Diem's plan to have a state-owned cigarette factory in South Vietnam was branded socialistic by American aid officials and denied development funds.

The free-world model brought with it an infra-structure that was aimed at servicing the penetration of Western capitalism and facilitating the work of the foreign investor and exporter—not at laying the groundwork for local economic takeoff. Such growth is perverse and disorienting to a people, and creates false models for cultural emulation.

The LDCs within the free-world orbit now import significant quantities of underarm spray, herbal essence shampoo, Schick razors and Kleenex, while they have not been able to significantly increase their per capita food supply. This did not happen as a result of freedom of consumer choice, but rather of cultural imperialism. It just happens that in this case the high culture of the mother country is not Catholicism, ballet, or cricket, but rather consumerism per se. Here, though, the distortion of this culture becomes magnified a thousandfold by the poverty and inequality of the have-not recipients of our largesse. We take their resources to make our junk, give them a very small fraction of this junk for even more of their resources, and make even more junk. It is in this manner that the economy of waste is internationalized.

Consider that F. W. Woolworth has over three billion in sales abroad (82 percent of that company's profits). All the Woolworths you've seen throughout America, selling all those gadgets, only account for 18 percent of their profit. In other words, their presence here is nothing compared to their presence in the rest of the world. Gillette's figures are less sensational. Only 55 percent of their profits come from abroad, the same as Coca-Cola which sells almost two billion dollars worth of its wares outside the U.S., while Ford's "better idea" nets them over twenty billion dollars in foreign sales.[5]

So you've got a lot of cars and razor blades circling the globe. Tourism is up and there's even satellite transmission of our hottest television items (not to mention the domination of the foreign film and TV series markets). With jet travel and electronic photo transmission we have a shrinking world. Right? Wrong. Because in terms of the real stuff of people's daily existence (how much bread they get to eat, whether they have flush toilets, how many people sleep in a room, and is the place lighted) they are further away from us than ever.

If there is any area in which foreign aid has attempted to make a concerted input, it is that of food production, for everyone's interests it is hoped are served by there being less starvation in the world. Yet as the following data from the UN Food and Agricultural Organization attests, the results have been dismal. African food production per capita dipped during the last ten years and ended up slightly above where it started. Latin America, doing somewhat better, improved by a scant 4 percent in 1971 over 1960, but registered no progress at all from 1966 to 1971. The Far East (excluding China) hovered around the same point and the Near East did only slightly better, though it declined in more recent years.[6] In no sense can one speak of perceptible progress in per capita food supplies available to the have-nots. If we throw into the equation the growing income disparity that Secretary Rogers noted within the Third World, then assuredly there was significantly less food available per person on the lower end of the income scale at the end of the sixties than at the beginning. And the sixties were proclaimed by President Kennedy, among others, to be the development decade.

If we look at per capita GNP figures we can get some sense of the Third World people's command over world resources. GNP accounts, of course, are arbitrary assessments of economic worth in many senses, but the brute fact remains that a country's ability to garner world resources for its own purposes roughly corresponds to its percentage of the world's product. In 1971, Third World figures ranged from India's $91 per person per year to Chile's $632. The United States, by contrast, in that year registered a per capita GNP of $5,051.[7] If income were equally distributed within the various countries this would mean that each person in India could command roughly ninety-one dollars of the world's resources per year, while an individual in the U.S. could command over five thousand dollars worth. That is roughly fifty-five times as much.

Even if the Indians used these resources in a perfectly frugal and efficient manner, they would be up against the fact that they are dealing with a very small fraction of what's up for grabs. Any waste or frugality that they engage in is of marginal significance to the world's use of resources. Certainly this is so on a per person basis, but even as a nation, India clearly doesn't matter very much in world consumption accounts—*nuclear weapons or not.*

This can be illustrated in more concrete terms
through reference to consumption of various items
related to industrialization, as reported in the 1973
UN yearbook. Perhaps the most important index of
economic development is steel consumption, a key
element in virtually all industrial and transportation
activity. The United States consumes 617 kilograms
of steel per person annually, as compared to a scant
6 kilograms per person in Tanzania, Sudan, Pakistan,
Vietnam, and Bolivia. Indonesia does worse with 4,
and Afghanistan with 1, while India manages 14
kilograms, and a more advanced country like Chile
uses 77 which is still a small fraction of U.S. consumption.[8] The lesson for the conservation of resources is
again quite clear. Most of the world's people consume
an infinitesimal percentage of the ingredients that
make up steel.

The same proportions apply to telephone usage.
Whereas we in the U.S. get by on sixty phones per
hundred people, there are only two-tenths of a phone
per hundred people in India, and only slightly more
than that in Bolivia, Kenya, and the Philippines.[9]
It is not clear what the optimal number of phones
would be, but certainly the U.S. economy has ap-
propriated an incredibly larger percentage of the
resources needed for phone service (including energy) than other countries.

Finally, let's look at housing. We have .6 persons
per room in the U.S. (a little less than two rooms per
person), while in India there are over two and a half
persons to a room. Of our homes, 96 percent have

flush toilets inside, 97 percent have inside water, and virtually all have electricity. In Iran only 13 percent of the homes have inside water. As of 1960, 28 percent of homes in South Korea had electricity and 0.2 percent had flush toilets.[10] And both "oil-rich" Iran and South Korea are often held up as examples of miraculous economic development.

People in the LDCs simply do not occupy the same economic world as Americans in terms of consumption of finished products. They do, however, furnish raw materials for consumption elsewhere—not a very different reality than under old-fashioned colonialism. In the next decades this contradiction will intensify as the developed countries become more dependent upon Third World resources.

Just how dependent is a matter of some controversy, but there is no question, as Secretary of State Rogers' quote at the beginning of this chapter indicates, that the Third World will play a crucial and increasing role in the provision of resources beyond the much-publicized case of petroleum.

No less an authority on economic development than W. W. Rostow told Congress in justifying the foreign adventures of the Johnson years that "The location, natural resources and population of the underdeveloped areas are such that, should they become effectively attached to the Communist bloc, the United States would become the second power in the world."[11]

The Third World produces 52 percent of the world's antimony ore with most of the rest being found in the socialist countries. It produces 59 percent of the world's bauxite (the basis of aluminum production), and 94 percent of its chrome ore. The Third World is the basic source of tin (95 percent of the world production) and cobalt ore (72 percent of the world total). It contributes 45 percent of manganese ore production, and about a quarter of its lead and zinc.[12]

For those who hate statistics, what this all means is that much of the stuff needed for modern industrial processes has to be shipped from poorer sections of the world to richer ones. *Preservation of those supply lines has been a key element of our foreign policy in the past, but in the future, as the U.S. further depletes its own resources, this will become a virtual obsession.* As *Fortune* magazine pointed out recently:

> There is certainly abundant physical evidence that the U.S., at least, may already have creamed off its best metallic resources. As a consequence, American industry has been turning increasingly to foreign sources. A net exporter of raw materials until World War II, the U.S. has been an importer ever since, and the trade gap is widening. In 1970 the U.S. metal industry met less than 60% of its primary demand with domestic ores. The growing use of foreign ore places the U.S. in competition for the available supply with the rest of the world where demand for metal has been soaring.[13]

This competition is a growing source of tension between the U.S. and other capitalist powers, with the Third World the inevitable bone of contention. There has been much publicity given to studies like MIT's Club of Rome report which point to actual depletion of key nonrenewable resources in this century. But there are two short-run implications of the resource drain that have more pressing implications for Third World economic development.

To begin with, Third World development is never considered as a serious factor in projections of future resource consumption. It is generally assumed by most analysts, and one cannot fault their grim realism, that the Third World is going to plod along at its current rate. A serious rise in Third World use of their own resources in their own industrial production would very much heighten the world's resource crisis. Such development is a direct threat to the interests of the waste economies, unless the international economic order experiences a fundamental revolution and begins to allocate scarce resources on the basis of some sense of human need and social justice, rather than corporate and national competition. If this does not happen the developed countries will be under great competitive pressure to thwart Third World development without even the luxury of pretending to be interested in aid. Talk around the energy crisis already carries this flavor—if they won't sell it to us at a "reasonable price" we'll have to take other steps to ensure supplies, etc. Shades of Teddy Roosevelt.

Another implication of the resource push relates to the Third World's future access to materials for their own development through ordinary market mechanisms. The basic effect of the "creaming" of the highest grade ores is to drive up the price for metals. At first glance, this may seem a boon to poorer countries in the business of exporting resources. But it is not, unless a country is very richly endowed, very underpopulated, and is content to remain simply a producer of resources. Kuwait is a country apparently with such options but even oil-producing Iran has too big a population base for this. Her oil revenues must be reinvested as part of an industrialization process to improve the standard of living significantly. Even Kuwait and Saudi Arabia must cater to the question of general Arab economic development, or experience great instability and eventual takeover by poorer, but more populous neighbors. In any case, oil does run out, and past receipts left in foreign bank holdings and stocks have a way of evaporating or being absconded with by deposed rulers. They are hardly a sound basis for a national economy. Both Kuwait and Saudi Arabia have been forced to recognize this reality, and have responded to Arab pressures with token loans and aid programs as well as development programs in their own territory. And if the oil countries can't go it on resource export alone, then no country can. So, while rising resource prices may temporarily bring in more cash, it must be used for development.

It is precisely in this matter of development that the rise in resource prices backlashes against the poorer countries. First, they must pay a higher price for finished machines and other industrial goods that they must import for their development. As the jump in gas prices reveals, multinational companies are very skilled in passing on more than the increased resource cost to the consumers. Being vertically integrated, they most often control the finished product themselves, and are capable of acting in consort with other multinationals. These gentlemen's agreements are beyond the control of the poorer nations who are pitted one against the other and forced to play the monopolies' ball game.

This is true even when the Third World country does not buy finished goods but simply wants the raw materials. She will most often have to buy them from a multinational at a big markup.

Fortune magazine specializes in bright-faced optimistic responses to any talk of crisis. In that spirit they reminded the reader that, "The outcome projected in *The Limits to Growth*, the MIT Club of Rome study, with world industry 'overshooting' its resource limits and abruptly collapsing, ignores the capacity of the market system to stretch the supply through price increases."[14] This may be of some consolation to the most developed countries, but those higher prices will leave poorer countries that much further out in the cold.

part three

VISIONS
OF FREEDOM
AND WASTE

chapter 9

FOREIGN AID: END OF AN ILLUSION

The Kissinger strategy, like that of the MIT Club of Rome report, assumed the continued economic stagnation of the Third World as an unchangeable given. The current thinking of the Republican administration is that foreign aid does not even have to be maintained, let alone developed as a serious weapon for economic growth. With the exception of the oil kingdoms and a few "miracle" countries such as Brazil, Taiwan, and South Korea, U.S. policy assumes a growing poverty gap in Third World countries and a smaller proportionate commitment to development on our part than previously. They will stagnate, we will grow, and if they are unhappy with that state of affairs their only recourse is to create more favorable conditions of investment for multinational corporations—such is the "self-reliance" of the Nixon legacy.

World Bank chairman Robert McNamara predicts that India will have a per capita income of two hundred dollars by the end of this century, when that of the average citizen in the U.S. will be over ten thousand dollars.[1] But that's only if India gets her hands on the minimal capital needed to increase her export manufacturing sectors and decrease her dependency on agricultural exports.

Given their low starting economic base and population increases, it is unrealistic to expect most Third World economies to very seriously increase capital investment in manufacturing, short of the strenuous efforts of a centrally planned economy accompanied by the sort of revolutionary fervor witnessed in China. Even then the poorer countries will remain hungry for capital to fulfill development plans, particularly for hard foreign-exchange currency to import sophisticated machinery. For the noncommunist countries, that can realistically be expected to come from only two sources—private foreign investment or official government assistance. Recent U.S. foreign policy has been clearly one of deemphasizing the latter while rapidly increasing the former.

Not the least of the various problems associated with private investment is that it ends up extracting more capital than it puts in, and perhaps more importantly, takes decision-making out of the hands of the developing country. But Third World countries have been forced to scramble for such investment by the multinationals because of the refusal of the developed countries to provide them with serious amounts of capital on a government-to-government loan basis. By starving them for official low-interest capital, they force a dependence upon the multinationals.

In the case of the U.S., while private investments by U.S. companies in the Third World have dramatically risen (as a percent of the GNP), official aid through the World Bank has been in relative decline. McNamara, former Defense Secretary and current head of the World Bank, put it this way;

> The contribution from the United States . . . continues to decline. It has already fallen from above .5 percent of GNP in the early years of the last decade to .31 percent in 1970. It is likely to fall further to around .24 percent by 1975.[2]

McNamara went on to show that this failure of the developed countries to meet even the minimal aid (which he calls "ODA flows") that had been promised to the UN General Assembly would create a crisis situation for the poorer countries.

> The truth is that if ODA flows level off at substantially less than the target for the decade, (.7 of GNP) mounting debt problems for the developing world are inevitable. In the face of an ODA deficit, the developing countries would either have to reduce their rates of growth or increase their debts above reasonable levels. They are likely to do both.
>
> Since the mid-1950's, publicly guaranteed debt has been growing at about fourteen per cent a year. At the end of 1972 it stood at about $75 billion. Servicing of debt rose by eighteen per cent in 1970 and by twenty per cent in 1971. The average rate of increase since the 1960's had been about twice the rate at which export earnings, from which debt must be serviced, have been growing. Such a relationship cannot continue indefinitely.[8]

For the situation to get better, export earnings would have to be growing faster than the payment of interest on past loans. Instead they are falling behind. In a real sense then, the poorer countries, in a bind similar to that of ghetto inhabitants in the rich countries, are running twice as fast to stand still. McNamara doesn't explore one obvious option which would be for the richer countries to simply forget about the past debts and, at the same time, infuse massive new amounts of capital. Let's say the U.S.

were to up its contribution from the present three billion to twenty-three billion (or from one-fourth of one percent of our GNP to two percent). This would bring the amount of development aid up to the level currently spent on advertising in this country, not a far-fetched analogy given that the main justification for advertising expenditures is that they create new markets. Certainly economic development in the Third World would do likewise. Would such spending be extreme? And yet it is McNamara who has told us:

> The gap between the rich and the poor nations is no longer merely a gap. It is a chasm. On one side are nations of the West that enjoy per capita incomes in the $3,000–$5,000 range. And on the other are nations in Asia and Africa that struggle to survive on per capita incomes of less than $100.[4]

It is simply inconsistent to talk of the problem in terms of a chasm and the solution in tenths of a decimal point increases in aid. This level of aid is what McNamara at another point refers to as "window-dressing" and not a serious contribution to development.

If we look at another resource allocation, military spending, we can find a more serious commitment. As McNamara states: "The world is spending $183 billion a year [in 1970] for armaments—a sum twenty-four times larger than the total spent on all foreign assistance programs."[5]

Robert McNamara has lived a good part of his

adult life on the high peaks of American power. He was president of the Ford Motor Company, and later Secretary of Defense. He seems possessed of a unique ability to internalize the goals of whatever institution he is working in, and so we should not doubt his present desire as head of the World Bank to "do something" about world poverty, any more than we would have formerly doubted his desire to increase the output of larger and larger autos, and then larger and larger bombs. But he is most disappointing as a source of information on why America does not contribute more toward economic development in the Third World. Where he was successful at procurement and growth in his other roles, in his current job he is failing his sales targets. But why? His answer is a strange one in that it tells us everything and yet nothing about this dilemma.

> . . . . There is no lack of capacity in the American economy. . . . What may be lacking is a broad commitment of the national will. . . . Or perhaps the lack is not so much our national will as a lack of understanding—or not so much a case of indifference to responsibility as a case of understandable confusion over the competing claims on attention and national resolve.[6]

Now Robert McNamara is a man normally accustomed to the exactness of computer printouts, and, indeed, when he discusses the economic problems of development he is given to great precision of language. But what is this business of "commitment" and "national will" or "confusion"? Whose confusion and why? Why is there no confusion about competing claims for the military budget or oil depletion allowances? Better yet, what has the national will ever had to do with oil depletion allowances? Most Americans haven't the vaguest idea of how much of our aid is military and how much developmental, for the figures have been hopelessly and deliberately meshed together. Can there be any question that if the top fifty corporations had found foreign aid to be necessary to creating a sound business environment abroad it would have been dispensed in great doses, just as military spending is?

This sort of nonanalysis becomes totally ludicrous when McNamara attempts to deal with the more basic problems of the consumer society in the context of this "national will." Here is something he knows about very well, yet to speak of our national desire to consume apart from the growth and profit motives of American corporations and their accompanying armies of advertisers, designers, market researchers, ad nauseum, does not befit a man of intelligence. It's the old problem of powerful Americans becoming moronic in *public* discussion of political economy because they are unwilling to talk about decision-making and power within the American political system. How else are we to read the following, part of a very moving passage of concern about world poverty:

> What is certainly true is that the decision to respond both to pressures of domestic problems and to the

urgency of essential foreign assistance is, in the end,
dependent on the response to a far more basic and
searching question—a question that must be faced
not in the United States alone but in every wealthy,
industrialized country of the world. That question
is this: Which is ultimately more in a nation's interest: to funnel national resources into an endlessly
spiraling consumer economy (in effect, a pursuit of
consumer gadgetry with all its by-products of waste
and pollution); or to dedicate a more reasonable
share of those same resources to improving the fundamental quality of life both at home and abroad?[7]

This comes from the man who gave us the Edsel.
When did we as a nation *decide* to spiral endlessly?
Has this ever been an issue in our political life,
something Presidential candidates debated? Or has it
rather been the inevitable working of a system of
monopoly capitalism which, as we were told by another auto company president turned Cabinet official,
was as good for us as it was for General Motors. It
is good that McNamara can now see some signs of
the thing going haywire but his attempt to shift
responsibility for all that to our national will is
deliberately disorienting. If it is this consumerism
which is the main cause of waste and misappropriation
of resources in the world, then let's go to the roots
of consumerism rather than to the consumer. Mc-
Namara understands full well that we have left the
age of neo-classical competitive economy with its
sovereign consumers. He's been at enough sales meetings to know more accurately the power relation of
corporation to consumer.

What chance did the consumer ever have against

the marketing and sales forces of the big auto companies? None at all when we consider that most of
today's consumers were raised in a Cold War environment in which even raising questions about corporate
manipulation was subversive. With the exception of
a few muckrakers, like C. Wright Mills and Vance
Packard, there was virtual unanimity, even in academic departments of economics, on celebrating "the
invisible hand" of corporate power. We also know
that it is only recently that people like Nader have
been able to confront the corporations and withstand
their smear campaigns because the waste and pollution problems have gotten so out of hand as to obviously mock corporate propaganda of the good life.

We have come to regard as "necessities," things
which we never would have wanted were we in our
right minds. But we, as consumers, have not been in
our right minds for some time, while salesmen have
had control of our culture. They did not have to seize
that power. It just flowed naturally from the power
which the corporations had seized.

Indeed, the advertising agencies themselves have
become "multinational." According to *Advertising
Age*, the industry "bible," "If there is one development which stands out among all others in the
past decade of hectic activity in international advertising, it is the forging of giant multinational
agency conglomerates."[8]

Surely McNamara understands quite well that
growth as a goal does not have an independent existence in our national psyche. Growth, sales, profit,

and market research are all part of an essential logic which determines whether someone like McNamara will rise successfully within a company and, of course, whether the company itself rises or declines. As a sound businessman, he must also understand that corporations spend all of that money on sales promotion precisely because we, as consumers, are not naturally falling all over ourselves to get the latest item. Last year the six top auto makers spent almost half a billion dollars selling us cars which most of us now realize we didn't need.[9] But that half billion is only a small fraction of the money spent on style changes, design, market research, sales promotion, etc., also aimed at getting us to buy the cars. And all of that is only a fraction of the resources wasted on the actual production and operation of cars which we would not have felt a need for if they hadn't spent so much money on the sales promotion in the first place.

If McNamara is right in his assumption that one cannot deal with the growing crisis between the haves and have-nots in this world without talking about "consumer gadgetry," then one has to go a step further and say you cannot talk about consumer gadgetry without talking about corporate capitalism. If the resources of the world's people are being wasted on junk, then we have to talk about the process of manipulation which left Americans, with their rich tradition of self-reliance and freedom, consuming 50 percent of the world's resources when they are 6 percent of its population.

Whether we want to address these questions or

not, the reality of growing world conflict is forcing us
to. The fuel shortage did what no amount of moral
pleading, radical rhetoric, and antimaterialist folk-
singing could ever have accomplished—it forced
Americans, from truckdrivers to Cabinet members,
to think critically about the basic values of this nation's economic system. It was as if the system was
forced to turn on itself, with nightly television advertising alternately exhorting us to save energy by
not using so many gadgets, and moments later doing
everything it could to get us to buy more of them.
To buy a Cadillac as a way of conserving energy may
have made sense to some creative director of an ad
agency, but it's the sort of thing that produces psychic
disorder in the citizenry.

As the crisis of fuel became also a crisis of news-
print, and of zinc and of bauxite, the boom of the
seventies began to falter and the talk turned to reces-
sion rather than growth. In that atmosphere we have
begun to witness uglier currents of chauvinism toward the Third World. And, indeed, who is responsible? If it's either the consumer or the Arabs, the
consumer is going to be certain the Arabs are responsible, because consumers know that they are not
in the saddle. The Advertising Council, the World
Bank, the President's advisers, and even the nightly
newscasters who are so good on some questions of
marginal corruption and so poor on more basic ones,
were not about to point the finger where it belonged
—at the way our economy is organized, with its corporate power structure, decision-making, rewards,

sales, and, in the final sense, political input to our system.

The convenient separation of economics from politics has also taken major decisions as to the allocation of resources out of any democratically accountable process. To view the workings of the large corporations, domestically or internationally, as apolitical is to make "politics" irrelevant. To discuss poverty or smog in America or the Third World without centering on the dominance of corporate power (largely American) is simply an effort to obscure the key issues.

Much of the literature on world poverty assumes that the world of the poor exists in not so splendid isolation from that of the developed world. Their poverty is presumed to be a condition of their past history, as manifested in current cultural indexes of illiteracy, low technological skills, undisciplined work forces, and sharp internal religious and tribal differences. The link between us and them is most often presented as one of moral concern—we should help "save the little children" or some such appeal. It is conceded that the advanced countries have sometimes blundered into the world of the poor as in the bad old days of colonialism, or more recently a Vietnam, and that this certainly didn't help matters. But there is general agreement in both popular and academic writing that these political and military "errors" have little causal connection with the state of underdevelopment. They are, on the contrary, most often viewed as the products of misguided and overzealous do-gooder efforts by the developed countries. The instances of more blatant resource ripoffs are seen as exceptional, sporadic, and, however unfortunate, not basic to the malfunctioning of Third World economies. Indeed, they are presumed helpful in raising wage scales and cultural expectations. The links between the haves and have-nots are seen as marginal and accidental, and the only pragmatic "need" admitted is a fear that all of those hungry people might someday demand entrance to eat at our more bountiful table. Therefore, "for the sake of world peace and stability," we'd best help them. Which is all just so much rationalization for a situation in which "our" companies play a decisive role in maintaining this poverty. And the world "détente" which we are building is aimed at preserving that relationship—with the acquiescense of the Soviet Union. By failing to make the necessary commitment of public funds we have further enhanced the initiative of the companies which helped create the problems.

The most authoritative academic studies of the multinationals have been those of the Harvard Business School, which has also been sympathetic to their growth. Raymond Vernon, that project's director and certainly the leading university authority on the multinationals, offered the following summary of the project's findings on the impact of multinationals for the Third World:

> Contrary to general impression, there was a great burst of activity on the part of U.S. parents during

the twenty-odd years following the end of World War
II, in the establishment of manufacturing subsidiaries
in less developed areas. By 1967, the total investment
figure had gone up to $6.3 billion . . .[10]

The key to this expansion in manufacturing was
the "attractiveness of using well-disciplined, hard-
working, unskilled labor to perform standardized
tasks . . ."[11]

At first this investment was intended to produce
primarily for the local market, but with declining
overall costs, production in the Third World for export has become increasingly appealing. As Vernon
put it:

> The effect of employing the less developed areas for
> the export of manufactured products has begun to be
> apparent in the trade data reported from various
> countries. A comprehensive study covering Latin
> America, conducted by the U.S. Department of Com-
> merce for 1966, indicates that about 41 per cent of
> the exports of manufactured products from Latin
> American countries in that year were accounted for
> by the local subsidiaries of U.S. enterprises, even
> though the proportion of total manufactures of those
> enterprises in the area amounted to only 10 per
> cent.[12]

Vernon observed this to be a world-wide phenomenon and concluded that: "Increasingly, the destina-
tions of the products have been the markets of
advanced countries . . ."[13] He continued: "There
is not much doubt about the generalization to be
drawn from this data. The less developed world is

now well within the planning horizons of U.S. parents and within the logistical systems they have developed."[14] But he also warned of the potential competition from other nations' multinational companies.

One measure of the significance of this is the control it invests in the multinational company over finances and labor power in host countries, be they developed or not. Vernon's estimate is that "for every dollar that moves from the United States to foreign countries in connection with the financing of overseas manufacturing subsidiaries, something like three or four dollars are raised for those subsidiaries outside the United States."[15] Needless to say, the same thing is true of manpower: the 49,000 Americans employed in U.S.-controlled foreign subsidiaries in 1966 appear to have been:

> . . . associated with the employment of some 5.5 million local workers. Therefore the real value of the subsidiary, whether to the U.S. economy or to the host country, can hardly be measured by reference to the size of the capital sum that happened to cross the U.S. borders at the time of its establishment. The real value has to be measured by determining the marginal consequences of setting up the subsidiary, attaching it to the multinational enterprise, and putting its complex mixture of foreign and local resources to work as part of the global structure.[16]

We are then talking about something very different than government loans or private lending or portfolio investments in another country (which is the bulk of foreign capital coming to the U.S.). The multinational corporation is different precisely in that it practices a form of direct investment which leaves a measure of significant control over pricing, sales, wages, and investment decisions in the hands of the parent company. It is a mechanism for domination far more complete, albeit subtle, than earlier forms of neo-colonialism. But this passing of the world political and economic initiative to the multinational corporations is the essence of the Kissinger strategy in actual practice.

chapter 10

ASIAN DOLLAR A DAY

As our foreign policy passes into the hands of the multinationals it is fitting that we inquire more fully into their vision, which is often presented as the embodiment of variety and spontaneity—the antithesis of a puritanism found elsewhere. It is also the proudest claim of these companies to have brought job prospects and modernity to replace squalor and despair. And there are indeed jobs to be had.

After decades of protecting the "free sectors" of Asia from the asserted menace of the "blue ants of Mao's China," it seems that the West has come up with its own version of an ant society—according to a recent *Wall Street Journal* report on Western factories in Asia:

> Girls in the blue uniform of Hewlett-Packard Co. stream through one gate in the chain-link fence that surrounds the factories. Through another go the girls in the colorful batik print of Intel Corp. Others flock to work benches of National Semiconductor Corp., Hitachi Ltd., International Telephone and Telegraph Corp., and a dozen other companies.
>
> It's clear that this is where the industrial action is in Asia nowadays, and there is a simple reason: people.
>
> Electronics companies depend on hundreds, sometimes thousands of young girls to do the painstaking job of assembling tiny parts that are shipped home for use in computers and other products. Labor sometimes represents as much as half the cost of these parts, so the cheaper the labor the higher the profit. And here in Malaysia is where the cheapest labor can be found these days.[1]

This search for cheap labor by the electronics industry has brought Motorola to South Korea and General Electric to Taiwan, where components are made, shipped to Mexico for reassembly, and then sold in the developed world. On August 17, 1974, *The New York Times* offered an even more depressing account of the situation in South Korea. An article titled "South Korea Keeps Labor Costs Down Through Exploitation of Work Force" quotes an American priest: "Someone has to pay for all this development, and in Korea it is the workers."[2]

The use of this "cheap," primarily female labor power is the economic basis of the so-called miracle boom experienced by some of the smaller Asian countries, those most loyal in the past to America's Cold War posture and, hence, most secure for America's multinational corporations. But a corporation does not necessarily stay indefinitely in a particular country. Once labor rates have risen to the unreasonable sum of a dollar a day, it's time to expand elsewhere. As the same *Wall Street Journal* article traced this movement:

> The first big wave of electronics companies hit Asia about a decade ago, but those companies settled in such places as Hong Kong, South Korea, Taiwan and Singapore. At the time, those spots had hordes of unemployed, easily trainable workers. But that is no longer the situation—labor is becoming scarce and costly in those locales, so the companies now are looking elsewhere, mostly southward, mostly to Malaysia and occasionally to Indonesia.[3]

That this "costly" labor is a source of some concern gives us an indication as to just what kind of
"development" the multinationals have in mind. As
the *Wall Street Journal* article continued:

> "Hong Kong has gone up rapidly in wages, Taiwan
> is going up and Singapore is quite high," says an
> American executive in Malaysia. Starting wages on
> an assembly line in Taiwan now are $1.05 a day; in
> Indonesia, the pay is as low as 30¢ a day.[4]

Thanks be to the CIA for that timely coup against
Sukarno which kept Indonesia (with its oil) in the
ranks of the free world. Apparently the business community genuinely believes that entry into the world
of capitalist production and consumption is the *sine
qua non* of modern freedom. The writer of the above
quoted article did not intend to reflect poorly on
the activities of the American business community
in Malaysia. Nor did a subsequent article by E.
B. Weiss in *Advertising Age,* which later reprinted
those sections as the basis for a feature titled "The
Third World Starts Emerging as a Big Consumer Market,"[5] telling us the good news that the
new industrialization was tearing apart the restrictions of tradition and leaving the Third World ripe
for consumer goods and Western-style advertising:

> The people of these nations will tend to offer con-
> sumer goods, marketing the most dynamic growth
> potentials of the various export markets of the world
> during the on-coming decade—and, for some product

classifications, an even faster growing market than
the domestic market. Already the family car and 25"
color TV (as in Taiwan) are nudging out the traditional status symbol, the sewing machine.[6]

Malaysia provides a textbook example for other
developing countries on how to secure the blessings
of civilization. There are fifty-three electronics firms
which have affiliate factories there. Just how Malaysia
came to be so lucky is explained by Weiss in that same
article in *Advertising Age:*

> Because electronics companies want free import of
> parts for assembly, Malaysia set up several free-trade
> zones for factories. Because the companies prefer to
> operate in three work turns, Malaysia amended the
> labor laws to allow all-night work. Because foreign
> companies like ownership, Malaysia abandoned its
> requirements for joint ventures. Because taxes can be
> a huge cost of doing business, Malaysia offers com-
> panies up to ten tax-free years.[7]

Well, there's your vision of freedom. If there are
no taxes or joint ownership, all that Malaysia gets
out of American investment is the privilege of having
its women work through the night for thirty cents an
hour and a lot of new skyscrapers. Has the quality of
life in Malaysia improved? A quote from a *New York
Times* report indicates some reason for doubt:

> With the cars and with the smokestacks of sprouting
> new factories has come pollution. The air over Kuala
> Lumpur, once clear and sweet with the scent of
> hibiscus and other tropical blossoms, is becoming
> monoxidous and hazy.[8]

But the *Advertising Age* article does not pause for such doubts. The author delights in "taking my aficionados on a fast tour of the markets that will be generated in the Third World." The tour begins with a Mrs. Jamila Hunum, a housewife on the fringe of this "explosion." The only thing we learn about her needs or aspirations is that her house contains a highly polished linoleum floor, hooked rugs, china knickknacks, calendars, a bowl of wax fruit, plastic flowers, and a TV. "Note that variety of possessions," he exclaims to prospective advertisers in the Malaysian market. "Even five years ago that three-room shack would have been bare of possessions. What possessions will it have five years from now? That is the key question, and I suggest you permit your imagination to soar when you attempt to answer it."[9]

Am I alone in reading into this the exaltation of rape? The *Advertising Age* author would no doubt be offended by such a description, viewing it all as an exercise in freedom and self-determination. But does one extend freedom by creating in the victim a desire to be abused? How many nights does one have to work in the Motorola plant to be able to get one of those TVs?—six hundred? And how many for a car?

But again, we would be seriously underestimating the potential impact of all this if we failed to take into account the spiritual enthusiasm of the missionary. The men of *Advertising Age*, "the national newspaper of marketing," believe that sales and marketing are the key to the good life, and they are bent on extending these blessings to the world, even if it should prove resistant to their pitch. In the spirit of the true believer, their response to the crisis brought on by the excesses is to accelerate. Not content with having helped to create the mania of growth and gadgetry within the U.S. and the resulting enormous waste of resources, they are now determined to make this mania global. The article states the problem accurately enough:

> It is estimated that 500,000,000 people, consuming at the typical U.S. rate, would require all the resources, including energy, produced by the entire world! (Western Europe, the U.S. and Japan with a total population somewhat over 600,000,000 probably consume, right now, well over 80% of all the resources produced by the rest of the world's population of several billion.)
>
> Those several billion are just now talking (and even demanding) more nearly equal rights, with respect to the consumption of resources, including all forms of energy.[10]

The demanding sounds like pretty rough stuff until you realize that this article puts the emphasis on consumption. What it projects is not some model of world-wide planning to utilize resources more effectively, but rather an intensification of the very process of waste through the same kind of individual consumption and marketing that created the problem in the advanced countries. Drunk on the prospect of sales, it is possible to mindlessly thrill to the "current rush to multiple car ownership, second homes, travel, etc." while conceding in the very next paragraph that all this "will add to the resource shortage problem."[11]

I have spent this much time on the *Advertising Age* article because I think it represents in its purest form the ideology of the sales ethic. The Advertising Council ads about saving energy by turning down the thermostat are simply PR. This is the real thing. And there can be no doubt about the accuracy of *Advertising Age*'s prediction for a certain sector of the Third World. Kids who do not have sufficient protein do feel freer drinking Pepsi Cola. There are thousands of young Asian women working miserable hours for pitifully low pay, in order to purchase TVs that will in turn convince them that they need to work even longer hours to purchase still other "necessities." And, yes, it must be conceded that the magic of advertising might just be sufficient that they will internalize its messages even when all of the appliances which they have painfully acquired cannot be used because of an energy shortage.

But there is a struggle between the "open" societies of the free world and the closed ones behind the Bamboo Curtain, no matter what else may have changed in the Cold War. For an individual in the open society is, by definition, first a consumer and only in the most minor sense a social being. The social alternatives that existed in traditional society have been destroyed; and new ones are not allowed to form, lest they become "creeping socialism" or communism. This is true to the extent that a society is pervaded by "market forces," an indication of the degree to which hopes and fantasies are bound up with the act of consumption.

The grand struggle for the minds of men and women particularly in the Third World, comes down to a choice between a multinational ad agency like J. Walter Thompson, with its $400,000,000 in international billings, or the Taichai People's Commune with its "serve the people wholeheartedly" wall-posters. And whatever reservations one may have about life on a people's commune, one should entertain the possibility that it provides for a more effective utilization of resources and a less alienated existence than do the aspirations pushed by the ad agencies.

Consumerism as a goal is not only unrealistic in some ultimate sense (in these times, ultimate is 1990) of an exhaustion of world resources; it is exactly the opposite of what is needed for Third World economic development. There is no doubt that one can provide the illusion of some development by flooding the middle-class shopping sections of the cities of the Third World with consumer goods. This is a phenomenon common to Seoul, Casablanca, and Bogota. But it is not development. On the contrary, it caters to the indulgence of a privileged sector who thereby squander needed capital in return for accommodating the needs of foreign investment, and holding down the mass of people or disorienting them from carrying out a genuine social revolution. In the event that the reader dismisses this as the ravings of a radical malcontent, let's turn again to Robert McNamara: "Increases in national income, as essential as they are, will not benefit the poor unless they reach the poor. They have not reached the poor to any significant degree in most developing countries in the past . . ."[12] As an illustration, he offers Brazil with its booming consumer economy and truly burgeoning middle class. In Brazil in the past decade, "the share of the national income received by the poorest 40 per cent of the population declined from 10 per cent in 1960 to 8 per cent in 1970, whereas the share of the richest 5 per cent grew from 29 per cent to 38 per cent during the same period. . . . The very rich did very well."[13]

Now I would submit it is precisely that top 5 percent that is benefiting from the increased consumerism in the Third World, and that poorer people are actually made worse-off by spending an increased portion of their meager income on junk. If people need more protein in their diets, what sense of morality can permit the introduction of electric carving knives and color TV? The imports of the top class are obviously competitive with the need to invest capital in more useful ventures. As Ivan Illich points out, for every Cadillac imported by a poor country, there could be a bus that would transport forty instead of one or two.

For those who think the skewed figures for Brazil are exceptional, McNamara offers figures for Mexico, another "miracle" country:

> Between 1950 and 1969 the average income per capita grew, in real terms by 3 per cent per year. The richest 10 per cent of the population received about

half of the total national income at the beginning of the period and an even larger share at the end of the period (49 per cent and 51 per cent). But the share of the poorest 40 per cent of the people, only 14 per cent in 1950, declined to 11 per cent in 1969. The share of the poorest 20 per cent during the same period sank from 6 per cent to 4 per cent . . .[14]

The intrusion of Western capitalism into the Third World, has, indeed, resulted in a changed and expanded middle and upper class, one geared more toward the changing fads of the Western consumer market than to traditional values. Perhaps for them, this is progress or even liberating. But the reality of Third World existence is that the vast majority of the people can only stare into the windows of the new shops.

Robert McNamara is certainly determined to put the best face on recent "development efforts," but the data is so overwhelming that even he must conclude that:

We are not talking here about a few maladjusted discontents. We are talking about hundreds of millions of desperately poor people throughout the whole of the developing world. We are talking about 40 per cent of entire populations. Development is simply not reaching them in any decisive degree. Their countries are growing in gross economic terms, but their individual lives are stagnating in human terms.[15]

The figure is 40 percent here rather than 80 only because McNamara is talking of the most underprivileged of rural folk, the "900 million whose annual incomes average less than $100."[16] In his world view, development has helped the young women in the blue uniforms working for a dollar a day in the Motorola factory who make up the more "cheerful statistics."

> Yet we all know that these cheerful statistics are cosmetics that conceal a far less cheerful picture in many countries. The oil-rich nations of the Middle East have prospered economically; so have some small states in East Asia. But, for the nations of Africa and South Asia—nations with a total population of over one billion—the average increase in national income is, at most, 3.9 per cent and much of the growth is concentrated in the industrial areas, while the peasant remains stuck in his immemorial poverty, living on the bare margin of subsistence.[17]

Cosmetics are what it's all about: face-lifting in certain sections of the key cities; modern air-conditioning; IBM computers in the offices of the juntas, and the best of dictating machines for secretaries of the new breed of lawyers who advise the multinationals. The problem with all this is that it exacerbates the tensions of poverty. It's one thing for the very rich of a poor country to go off somewhere (rich Cambodians in the old days went to the French Riviera) and quite another to carry on right there in home territory.

But consumerism is a powerful weapon for raising false consciousness or false expectations. And it is the essential wisdom of the multinational advertising agencies to understand the potential of credit purchases and the dreams of billboard advertising as a holding action. If a peasant family can manage to get one of its nieces a job with Westinghouse, then a little progress might seem just around the corner. This was the vision of Saigon during the worst days of the war—the promise of yellow Hondas and Cutty Sark to make you forget about the bombs nearby. What the admen know, and what the rest of us tend to forget, is that satisfaction will not be delivered. Instead the admen keep upping the ante, and when the due date arrives, they're not going to be around anyway. But this must also be the vision of the more respectable World Bank. It is quite clear that the solutions of the market economies have failed. But in a holding action it is in fact wise to share alarm at crises—hence World Bank reports may appear realistic and concerned about Third World people. Various "solutions" like curbing birth rates, or increasing exports through more foreign investment are suggested. It is the politics of muddling through, so accurately defined by Jules Feiffer. But even if it will not wash in the long run, it does not mean that it is not useful to people of power in the short run.

Consumerism is the other side of the World Bank's coin. Talk development; talk consumption; grab resources, cheap labor, and sales; and hope the natives don't get wise. When they do, buy off their leaders, or educate their leaders in the best of your schools. Dangle trinkets in front of the eyes of the masses and trust in the combined power of confusion and nuclear weaponry. Talk aid and investment (don't be the "ugly American"), learn their language, develop water pumps and miracle grains, help them in all the ways that are not threatening to your power—and all the time with the goal of keeping their society from "closing" to you. A "closed society" is the primitive trick of the natives—it leaves the snake oil salesman mute and with his hands bound. One quick antidote is to make the definition of freedom synonymous with that condition which guarantees to the snake oil salesman the right of free speech and unbound hands—a Third World where there is peaceful competition between a wretched traditional society and a wretched market society. If that's the only range of choice, then the people will opt for the market, the ultimate dream of a dollar a day, a TV in every home, and a car in every village, even if there are no roads or gas.

Be sure to make the alternative of communism appear dark, antireligious, primitive, unfree, antifamily, etc. Young and Rubicam is good at that—so is ITT. The communist revolutionaries are notoriously lousy at mass propaganda in the cities—they don't know the art of billboards and TV. They are most effective in the patient weal of the village—the slow testing of a rural people's war; the peasant underground, the continuous raising of political consciousness. They feed on traditional communal life, with its village solidarity, while the admen are good at the instant gratification of lonely individuals in the hell of the big city. This was the vision of the *Advertising Age* article, quoting the vision of *The New York*

Times that Malaysia would be saved for the forces of freedom because there was "already a migration of country boys to the city to seek their fortune in the new world of skyscrapers."[18]

While it is basically no different than the American dream, it is much more vicious in that it will be very much less realized. For whatever doubts we now have about consumerism as a way of life for the economically advanced countries, it should be quite clear that our consumerism has been a disaster for the Third World. To talk now of doing the same there is, as Marx said, to repeat history "the first time as tragedy and the second as farce." It is to reduce the indignity of poverty to bathos. To have a peasant woman in South Vietnam make it to the city to be a prostitute of one sort or another, change the shape of her eyes, the smell of her hair, to so disorient her sense of family and death as to leave her miming the stereotypic suburban American housewife (herself a victim), is not only to leave her aping banality, but a caricature of it.

It must now be doubly confusing to those who have paid this price to be saved by us from the horrors of Mao's communism, that Richard Nixon suddenly no longer found it quite so horrible, threatening, or offensive. The last hurrah of anticommunism left more than a few of the free-world faithful in our Asian outposts wondering what the struggle for freedom had been all about.

chapter 11

SOUTH KOREA:
THE GREAT
WHITE HOPE

While the U.S. State Department now concedes that the general economic condition of the Third World is very bleak, it nevertheless delights in turning to various bright spots of successful economic development. It is particularly enthusiastic about the "economic miracles" of Taiwan and South Korea as models to be followed by other countries. These models presumably show the positive effect of U.S. official aid and private investment by large corporations mixed with a free, nonsocialist economy.

The futurist Herman Kahn goes further in considering South Korea to be the most successful recent example of development in the Third World and predicts that by the next century it will have the twelfth strongest economy in the world.[1] Richard Nixon termed it a "vigorous" model of what other nations can do, and pointed with enthusiasm to the fact that "for the past four years the South Korea economy has grown at a remarkable average rate of more than 10%."[2]

The "success" of South Korea is in some ways truly impressive. Stagnation through the fifties, despite massive American aid, led to the disintegration of the Syngman Rhee regime and the seizure of power by a South Korean military junta. Since 1962 Park Chung Hee, the junta's strongman, has instituted a series of five-year plans projecting rapid economic growth on the basis of massive imports of foreign capital. As a result, the country's GNP has risen dramatically from $2.3 billion in 1960 to $9.5 billion in 1973.[3] And it is that figure which causes the authors of a survey for the Morgan Guaranty Bank to note: "With each passing year, the economy of South Korea commands more and more attention on the part of students of economic development."[4] The same survey attributes South Korea's "remarkable growth rate" to the "striking liberality of the country's investment laws," which among other things, permit 100 percent foreign ownership and a moratorium on taxes.[5]

The South Korean model is in many ways the best-foot-forward of American foreign political and economic policy. It is certainly, more than any other model, a creation of that foreign policy, beginning with the U.S. occupation at the end of World War II and the "Korean Conflict." The U.S. first underwrote Syngman Rhee with massive aid "as a democratic strongman" in Asia, then cast his successor Park in that same role.

In the fifties the regimes of Rhee, Ngo Dinh Diem in South Vietnam, and Chiang Kai-shek on Taiwan had been held up as the free world's alternative to communism, bringing economic development along with political democracy. By the beginning of the sixties, it was conceded that South Vietnam was not making progress on either count. We had given up on presenting Chiang as a democrat, but still boasted of his economic progress; and Rhee in South Korea was simply forlorn. With the Park coup, which the U.S. supported, the prospect of a democratic model of economic growth was temporarily revived. But the political component was soon dropped, as it became clear that the key element of the economic model was a military-controlled, hard-working, austere society in which students and other dissident elements which had toppled Rhee would no longer be a source of "instability."

That South Korea has emerged as one of the more repressive societies in the world is no longer in much doubt. The kidnapping in the fall of 1973 of opposition leader Kim Dae Jung by the South Korean CIA settled that. Kim Dae Jung had been billed in the Western press as the popular "Bobby Kennedy of South Korea" and when he was dragged from his Tokyo hotel room and spirited to Seoul it looked pretty bad.

In a letter to *The New York Times* on May 28, 1974, Professor Jerome A. Cohen, the Director of East Asian Legal Studies at Harvard University and a colleague from MIT noted:

> Americans have been told for nearly thirty years by our highest authorities that the purpose of American aid to Korea (now over $12 billion) was to defend democracy there. Yet South Korea today is not only no democratic state; its decrees mark it as more ferociously antidemocratic and intolerant of its citizens than is even the Soviet Union.[6]

But the argument for South Korea, as for the other military juntas supported by the U.S. in Chile, Brazil, etc., is that they represent an intermediate stage for a nation's economic development. Beginning with the Rockefeller report on Latin America, it has been openly argued that the U.S. should support such regimes as the only ones which could provide the framework for economic development. It is these regimes which have come to be the "viable" models pushed by the U.S.

Let's begin an examination of South Korea's model economy by noting that it is no great exaggeration to call South Korea a country turned into one big "free-trade zone." Whereas other countries have designated a portion of their territory to be used by foreign companies to assemble products with cheap local labor, tax-free South Korea has not only done that but has also offered the most extensive concessions or guarantees of this sort throughout the country. The key to her "growth" is first off making a cheap labor supply available to foreign investors. As the *Far Eastern Economic Review* reported:

> The major resource used for development was the country's large, literate and industrious labor force. In fact, South Korea has few other natural resources. A steady increase in the productive age group, movement from rural to urban centers and the drafting of women into the labor force as well as restrictions on wage increases and union activity kept a brake on labor costs.[7]

One of the restrictions on the labor force has been a blanket prohibition of strikes by employees of foreign corporations. The beneficial effects of all this were summed up by Canada's *Journal of Commerce* in glowing terms:

> Wage levels in the Republic of Korea are one-tenth of those in the U.S. and one-sixth of those in Japan. Koreans have gained a reputation of being efficient

and hard-working. So most Japanese and U.S. ventures in Korea are labor intensive.

There is no minimum wage. Strikes by employees of foreign companies are prohibited.[8]

Strongly reminiscent of the old days of the Shanghai concessions, foreign companies in South Korea are currently given a tax holiday of five years and a guarantee against government nationalization.

The key to this model of development is the maintenance of "a stable business climate" by a strong military government. Third World countries, which permit or tolerate union struggles, or threaten nationalization, or even serious taxation of foreign enterprises, cannot follow this model for that would not make for a good "investment climate." And this business of attracting foreign investment is a very competitive one.

For the sixties, investment in Korea appeared to be a good business deal because it was so locked into the U.S. and its junta ruled with a firm hand. But, in the seventies, Park ran into difficulties with his American and Japanese trading partners, and his ability to keep the lid on Korean workers has begun to be more and more tenuous. It is important for the "success" of South Korea that the benefits of increased production be passed on to the foreign investors and overseas consumers and not to local workers except in minor trickles. Otherwise it stops being a good labor market. A recent report in the *Far Eastern Economic Review* gives a clear view of what this "miraculous growth" of over a decade has meant for Korean workers:

> In the past, Korean workers have been docile towards their employers. However, the growing gap between rich and poor (the disparity between villas and tar-paper shacks) . . . is giving Korean workers a new sense of outrage and solidarity. . . .
>
> Because of this growing awareness and the fact that the average manufacturing wage is $40 a month, compared to the Bank of Korea's estimate that an urban family of four needs $90 a month for its expenses, wage demands can be expected to increase. This is especially true in textiles (Korea's largest export item) where young girls earn between $12 and $25 monthly for working ten hours a day six days a week.
>
> The foreign investor is concerned about rising wages (American electronic firms are now flocking to Malaysia rather than Korea) but not nearly as much as the Government.[9]

This concern of the Korean government can get quite brutal, as was demonstrated when the workers of the Daegwan Sanup textile factory dared to strike in March of 1973 and were dragged off by the police. "The workers had the temerity to strike although Lee Hu Rak (the head of South Korea's powerful CIA) is rumored to be on the company's board of directors," reported the *Far Eastern Economic Review*.[10] That's the same CIA which had Korea's "Bobby Kennedy" kidnapped—aptly demonstrating that planning skills developed in the public sector are equally useful in the private one.

Any small gains of the workers are consistently

wiped out by the rampant inflation which has been a constant feature of this "model." Wage increases of 8.8 percent have not been able to keep up with a rate of inflation equal to 10 or even 15 percent (as in 1971–72).[11] It is clear then that this model does not expect Korean workers to be the new consumer market for Korean products of the boom. Their cheap labor is used to assemble products primarily for the export market.

South Korean exports have jumped from a very low forty-one million dollars in 1961 at the start of the "boom" to over three billion dollars worth in 1973. *Fully one-third of the gross national product is intended for export.* These are mostly heavy labor-content products such as wigs, textiles, clothing, wood products, and electrical goods. In the years between 1962–72 these exports grew at a phenomenal rate of an average of 40 percent. In 1973 they jumped by 80 percent. But now important sectors in the domestic economy—in particular, agriculture—have stagnated or declined in this same period.[12]

The stark fact which now confronts the South Korean government is that her export economy has been floated for twenty years by the U.S. and that America is no longer willing to play that role.

In the fifties it had been primarily a matter of U.S. economic and military aid, which in the sixties was complemented by very extensive private and public loans as well as direct investment. Between 1946 and 1969, U.S. economic aid to South Korea exceeded that to South Vietnam and totaled $4.9 billion, which

when added to the $2.9 billion of military aid, pro-
vided an input of $7.8 billion.[13] The Vietnam war
was a particular bonanza for the South Korean economy, bringing in over a billion in remittances and
supports of various kinds.[14] But those glory days of
U.S. support are over. The U.S. ran into its own
balance-of-payments problems, developed protection-
ist sentiments and is playing for bigger Asian stakes
with its new China policy. South Korea no longer
retains its special usefulness as an American military
base on the periphery of China. Indeed, the subsequent shifts of policy brought on by the Nixon Doctrine have had a major effect on the South Korean
economy, which in 1971–72 was thrown into a down-
swing as a result of U.S. policies. The precarious
situation was only held together by the massive entrance of Japanese capitalism aimed at reasserting its
historic colonial influence. Whereas U.S. direct investment in 1973 had fallen to a mere two million,
that of the Japanese that year was seventy-five times
as much.[15]

This dependency on one or another foreign power
is built into the model of hothouse export growth
exhibited by South Korea. As *The Oriental Economist*
pointed out in 1971:

> In spite of its phenomenal success in setting ever new
> growth records in exports, or more likely because of
> it, Korea has become a precarious economy in which
> the growth creates an instability that is manageable
> only with continued growth. The trade gap remains

as big as ever and any slackening of export volume can bring a crisis in payments.[16]

Or as it was put more recently by another conservative source on Asian economics, the *Far Eastern Economic Review,* in its January 7, 1974 survey;

> The most important, and also the most difficult, problem for the Park Administration is the economy's almost total dependence on other countries. South Korea relies heavily on exports to lead its development, making the country particularly vulnerable to changes in world demand. Worse still it depends on the U.S. and Japan to take more than 70% of its exports, and many economists have predicted a downturn in the economies of both these countries.[17]

This dependency of the economy compels a preoccupation with the whims and priorities of the larger powers. If South Korea allows its workers' wages to increase, then U.S. manufacturers and importers will shift their operations to other areas as some U.S. firms already have done. South Korea is also heavily in debt to the U.S. and Japan, and must continually scramble to service that debt. The private and government loans which financed development have due dates which take an increasing share of needed funds for repayment. In the case of South Korea;

> The equity investments and loans produce increasing problems of repayment servicing. It has been estimated that debt repayment jumped to $360 million

> last year, a big chunk of export earnings. Further
> reducing the value of these earnings are the facts
> that a major part must go to pay for imported in-
> puts, while another slice is repatriated by foreign
> companies. It has also been suggested that the Gov-
> ernment's handsome export subsidies lessen the value
> to the country of the earnings.[18]

This problem is not restricted to South Korea but rather extends throughout the free-world development areas which have based their limited growth on such loans. A 1970 *Business Week* report on the World Bank meeting noted that the external public debt of developing countries has jumped fivefold since the mid-fifties and was growing at an average rate of 17 percent while income from exports was increasing by only 6 percent per year.[19]

The South Korean economy has shown little capacity to generate internal funds for investment. Its economy has come to be increasingly controlled by foreign capital which accounted for 40 percent of annual investment in the first two five-year plans, and will increase to a projected 60 percent in the third one.[20]

With the current economic restraints on the U.S. economy, and U.S. investment being attracted else-where, Japanese support becomes crucial. That support has a high price since Japan views South Korea very concretely as an appendix to its own economy for such necessary but undesirable production which has strained the space and air of Japan. The *Far Eastern Economic Review* noted that "Japan holds the lion's share of foreign investment, which totals $512 million, and is in a strong position to make South Korea's interests subservient to its own."[21]

The U.S. has many closer outlets for its pollution exportation, such as oil refining in Venezuela and Puerto Rico, but the nearness of Korea makes it more attractive to the Japanese for the things they are finding more difficult to do at home. As *Business Week* reported:

> "Most Japanese investments in Korea are labor-intensive and polluting industries," complains a Korean newspaper editor. "They cannot live in Japan, so they want to invest in Korea. We import pollution and labor exploitation. That does not help our economy much."[22]

This fits concretely into overall Japanese economic planning which goes a long way toward explaining the rapid revival of anti-Japanese feeling throughout Asia. As the magazine *Business Asia* summarized developing Japanese plans:

> Japanese interest will undoubtedly be further boosted by the proposed "international division of labor." Under this plan, Japanese labor-intensive industries that have reached marginal limits, as well as machine, metal and chemical industries with high pollution performance, would be relocated. Korea appears to be a logical relocation site for such industries.[23]

That even the higher echelons of the Korean government are wary of being an appendage to the Japanese economy is evidenced by their massive campaigns to call forth greater U.S. investment. Once a nation has taken this path of growth, it is locked into a never ending world of lesser-evil choices. It is a lesser evil to have direct investment than loans, and it is a lesser evil to have American investment (hopefully of cleaner technology) than Japanese or, at least, to balance the Japanese. Park is on a treadmill to keep the economy bubbling. In following this model he has to surrender more and more of his country's sovereignty in an attempt to win ever-larger amounts of investment, leaving his government ever more at the mercy of foreign "factors." Rising discontent within South Korea, manifested by demonstrations and the popularity of opposition candidates has scared off some U.S. investors. Again Park is caught in the inherent dilemma of this model—he was able to get the loans and investment in the first place because he suppressed the population and kept wages down, and now the population won't stay suppressed.

> As dissent boils up in South Korea, the Park Chung Hee regime finds itself caught in a political and economic vise: if it cannot continue to produce swift economic progress, unrest will undoubtedly spread beyond the student and intellectual sectors. The "economic miracle" of the past decade, however, is in danger of being obstructed. Undoubtedly the most ominous problem is the economy's almost total dependence on other countries. Unfortunately, and perhaps suicidally, the Government is countering this new situation not with the required economic solutions but by further social and political repression.[24]

This passage from a report in the *Far Eastern Economic Review* implies that the necessary solutions are somehow compatible with the economic model which the U.S. gave Park. But the deep trouble of the South Korean society is a direct result of that model.

The lopsided export development of South Korea, which permitted the ballooning of its GNP, has made a shambles of the rest of the economy. The most striking illustration of this is in the agricultural sector. Prior to the division of the country, the South was the rice basket for the nation, feeding the mountainous North as well as exporting. But since its "miracle" development, the South has become dependent upon massive food imports, while the North, which has followed an opposite model of economic growth under a socialist planned development, has become self-sufficient.[25]

South Korea's dependence upon outside food sources has been increasing dramatically even though the population growth rate has been under control. A failure of agricultural development rather than the "population problem" is at the root of the food crisis. (In fact, South Korea has had success in cutting its population growth down to 1.8 percent.) There has been an inverse ratio of shrinking agricultural yield against rising GNP and exports. In 1968, 247,000 tons of rice were imported, which rose to 631,000 in the next year and stayed at 539,000 in 1970. By 1971 it was over 800,000.[26]

The Oriental Economist of July 1973, after observing that dependence on foreign loans was the first distortion of South Korea's economy, added agriculture as the second;

> The second "distortion" is the stagnation of farming. Because of this shortcoming, the export industry has been the only sector manifesting growth, and there has been no upwelling of domestic consumption, while in 1972 it became necessary to import about a million tons of rice and wheat, roughly one-fourth of the amount produced in the country. The widening gap between farm and manufacturing incomes is becoming a serious social problem. One view has it that the Government fails to take up the farm problem in real earnest because much of the food imports consists of aid from Japan and the United States, and sale of this aid in kind results in revenue for government spending.[27]

But this last explanation misses the point. Imbalance is built into the model. And integrated social planning has never been one of the strong points of any capitalist society, developed or not. Indeed, South Korea has followed the example of the enclosure movements of English history: The countryside is thrown into disarray and masses of the peasantry are forced to move to the city, forming a reserve labor force of the type described by Marx in *Das Kapital*. In virtually every instance of free-world economic development, the swelling of the cities with a cheap supply of labor occurs, and tarpaper shacks are as common a scene in Santiago as Seoul. So, too, is unemployment, and a conservative estimate would place that of Seoul at 10 percent, which, again, is par for the course for this model.

Indeed, as recently as August 1974, *The New York Times* observed that: "By some estimates, about a million of these people live in slums, with little or no running water, with garbage rotting and with no guarantee that they won't be evicted for a new elevated highway or factory."[28]

Seoul does have a "new skyline" but the emphasis of new construction has been on hotels and industrial parks, whereas the ratio of population to hospital beds is one of the worst in the world. In 1971 there were 1,823 persons per hospital bed, as compared to 1,165 in Burma which is a much poorer country. For all its success in keeping down population growth, South Korea had a higher concentration of persons per hospital bed than India with 1,571.[29]

A U.S. Bureau of Labor Statistics report has documented the failure of South Korea to deal with diseases that are easily curable, such as polio, plague, typhus, scarlet fever, and smallpox. The labor force continues to be weakened by cholera, malaria, and parasitism.[30]

In 1970, while Nixon was frequently referring to the "remarkable model" of South Korea, his top pollution aid, Russell Train, visited that country on the last stop of a world tour. After visiting most of the other capitals, he reported that three cities were in the running for the title of most polluted—Seoul, Nationalist China's Taipei, and Turkey's Ankara. All three of these cities have been solidly in the free-world camp and the recipients of massive American aid and investment. Indeed, they may also be the three proudest achievements of the American model of development. So as not to play favorites, Train was cautious in judging the winner of the pollution contest. But according to *The Washington Post* account: " 'While the race is close and there are no agreed standards for choosing a winner,' Train said, 'Seoul would undoubtedly be my own nomination for first place. If it isn't there yet, it will be soon.' "[31]

The connection between this pollution and the pattern of foreign investment was obvious to the touring party of Americans, which included *The Washington Post*'s Selig Harrison, who noted:

> Many foreign investors make no secret of the fact that they are seeking to escape the threat of costly pollution control measures in their home countries, and Japanese motives are especially suspect here in the wake of 40 years of colonial rule.[32]

There has been much in the literature of economic development about the necessity to develop an infrastructure of publicly supported projects as a precondition for takeoff. But the problem with export development (and for some its virtue) is that it can get by with very uneven growth in the public sector. The South Korean government has been very efficient in the construction of industrial parks, expanding port facilities, and linking all that with a new network of modern highways. Its ports can handle large containerized tankers, and there is even a well-developed telephone system for industry as well as a whole series of modern "international-class" hotels to cover executive needs. These are the high-priority items, and, by this standard of industrialization, quite rightly so. But this really involves the creation of two economies—one for the needs of foreign investment and export trade, and the other, the nongrowth one, for most of the people. For the majority of the people, a tripling of the GNP has brought negative results in vital areas of their health, particularly in the cities which were presumed to be benefiting more from development; as discovered by Russell Train:

> Few areas of Seoul have sewers, and the task of developing a comprehensive sewage system is so overwhelming that officials plan to rely instead on septic tanks, cesspools and an expansion of the existing system of underground, outside "honey pots" where nightsoil is collected by municipal trucks.

> Contaminated water has periodically led to rampant cholera in some areas of Seoul and other cities. One of Train's advisers, who observed a key conduit point where the municipal drinking water supply enters the city, said that the water was "of a quality worse than what you would see in the New York City sewers."[33]

A final particularly obvious illustration of misallocation of resources from a social point of view is the inevitable example of the impact of the automobile industry on South Korea. During the rapid development of the sixties, Seoul did not even consider the planning of urban trains, and it wasn't until 1970, when traffic was barely able to move at peak times, that such efforts began—again much too late and too

little. The situation has become so extreme that even
J. W. Schneeberger, the manager of the local ESSO
office, stated that "70,000 cars are now fighting their
way through Seoul's jumbled hodgepodge of winding
old streets and busy new boulevards for fourteen
hours daily"[34] and that:

> Traffic will clearly continue to grow at a rapid pace
> and standards for pollution control should be for-
> mulated as quickly as possible to avoid disastrous
> consequences. Traffic density is so great here that the
> nitrogen oxide content in the air from auto exhaust
> is estimated to be five times greater than levels de-
> scribed as permissible in the U.S.[35]

With levels of pollution in the four main industrial
cities ten times higher than in New York City it was
amazing to the members of the Train mission that
the government was at best contemplating a "media-
tion council" to grant compensation awards to victims of pollution; "But the critics complain that
preventive medicine is what the country needs, and
point to the fact that the new national five-year plan
does not even mention pollution."[36]

The new five-year plan outlines a pattern of industrialization based on foreign dollars which will ac-
centuate all the problems to date. The plan is based
upon investments of foreign capital of ten billion
dollars between 1973 and 1981.[37] The paid supplement by the Korean government in *The New York
Times* (it was really the basis of a pathetic, prostrat-
ing appeal for foreign investment) stated that the
country would need "$3.99 billion in 1973–76 and

another $6.03 billion between 1977–81. Of the total of $10 billion, the government foresees $8.4 billion in loans and $1.6 billion in foreign investment."[38] It went on to note:

> This $10 billion is no small amount; as of 1972, Korea had obtained $3.45 billion during the ten-year period. This means Korea must obtain nearly three times more foreign capital than during the 1961–72 period in the nine years from 1973 to 1981.[39]

If there was ever a plan for economic development, dependent on foreign capital rather than internal development, this one is it. To get that sort of "support" requires the surrender of power over resource decisions to multinationals, pollution or not. So whatever may have been learned about the effects of traffic congestion, South Korea was very excited about the prospect of expanded auto production by Ford and GM. As *Business Asia* reported in 1972:

> General Motors Corp. (GM) will locate a major production facility in South Korea. . . . the joint venture will have an estimated initial capacity of 35,000 vehicles per year, which are intended for the domestic market.[40]

If 70,000 cars have already congested Seoul's streets, why not throw in another 35,000 and see what happens. If nothing else, the GNP will go up and that's what Park is after. It's the old adage with a new twist —what's good for GM is good for South Korea.

chapter 12

ECOLOGY
IN CHINA

Since Nixon's visit to China it has become somewhat fashionable to concede that although Mao's
adaption of Marxism is only of marginal interest to
those who live in the developed countries, it may be
all well and good for China. It is argued that China's
economic backwardness puts items high on its agenda
which have already been dealt with in the West, and
that we face newer postscarcity problems which the
Chinese will only come to know about after they
have developed.

The environmentalist movement has been given
to this insular view, and efforts to enlist the attention of writers on ecological matters to study
developments in China have had only minor impact.
Orville Schell, an environmentalist who is also a
Sinologist, has thrown down a basic challenge to
those interested in both areas, but has met with little
success. In an article in *Clear Creek* magazine he held:

> If the Chinese appear to have some solutions to im-
> pending world ecological disaster, it is not because
> they have sought to fine oil companies a paltry
> amount for each oil spill, not because they have
> slowly put better smog devices on private automo-
> biles, not because good citizens save their no-deposit,
> no-return bottles and cans, and not because people
> are worried that China is becoming ugly. Their solu-
> tions are direct extensions of the revolutionary na-
> ture of their social organization and value system.
>
> If the Chinese example tells us anything, it is that
> the environmental catastrophe which confronts our
> society will not be averted by band-aids or minor
> adjustments made at the top by the giant corporate

polluters, but by fundamental and often bold changes made in the whole way we as a nation produce.[1]

China has in recent years been swept by a campaign to implement "multipurpose" use, that is to turn waste products into useful ones. Schell quoted an article from the Chinese press about workers in Tientsin in a sulphuric acid plant who attempted to salvage steel from waste left in producing sulphuric acid:

> Many workers started multi-purpose use of waste after studying Chairman Mao's philosophical thinking. They came to understand that "all things invariably divide into two," and that under given conditions, waste materials could be transformed into useful things and the harmful into beneficial.[2]

Certainly a study of Mao's writings did not tell these workers precisely how to extract steel from the waste, but it did offer a political perspective on the word "waste"—its social implications and therefore its potential solution. A stream from a factory may yield a small percentage of a useful mineral which a private corporation would consider too small to warrant extraction for profit. But the social harm of that item remaining in the water may be very great and therefore extraction would be warranted. As an illustration, we find the example of the Kirin chemical industry:

> The dilute acid left over from production in the calcium carbide factory's acetic acid shop contained

> many important chemical materials, but was consid-
> ered of little economic value. The amount that could
> be recovered in a year in value does not even equal
> one day's output of the shop's main product. But
> this material discharged untreated as waste water
> pollutes the streams and the atmosphere. Constant
> contact with it irritates the nostrils and can result
> in damage to the nervous system.[3]

According to this account, the workers in the plant
proceeded to make equipment to recover the chemicals in the water, even though factory leaders thought
it not worth the outlay of funds:

> Socialist enterprises, they pointed out, should think of
> the people's welfare. True, recovering waste material
> called for additional equipment and state funds, and
> in that sense it looked like a "loss." But, they said,
> "What about the greater gain of preventing pollution
> and getting rid of health hazards?"[4]

My own travel in China was certainly too brief to
verify the specific press items quoted here. But there
is no doubt that the issues they deal with (if not the
particular details of their solution) are central to the
Chinese experience and form a key part of the differences with current Soviet communism. In the following accounts I have relied almost exclusively on reports
from the Chinese themselves, since foreign reportage
is still far too sketchy to provide verification or dis-
proof. But the Chinese have evolved an obvious "approach" toward the questions of growth, waste, and
consumerism which is startlingly different from our
own "way of life;" and is noticed by even the most

casual visitors. It seems useful indeed to examine their position on the key questions the world now faces.

Whether or not one accepts this rendition of the Mao-Liu/Soviet conflict, the fact remains that Mao has been consistently identified with the idea of organizing socialist society on a basis of political or moral incentives, while the Soviets have moved toward individual material incentive and profitability. From a social point of view, the diseconomies of this last sort of decision-making are by now well understood even in the West.

Mao's contention is that the raising of political consciousness is the key ingredient to building a socialist society *after* the seizure of power. This is an important addition to socialist thought and is basic to the functioning of the Chinese communist economy. Its environmental benefits seem obvious for they put social incentive to the fore, rather than making it a secondary consideration. It is Mao's contention that the Soviets have betrayed this essential point. *Peking Review* summed up the difference:

> During the Great Cultural Revolution, the plant's revolutionary committee organized all its staff members and workers to study Chairman Mao's teachings and mercilessly criticized the revisionist line, including trash like "making great efforts to do what is most profitable, less efforts to do what is less profitable and no efforts to do what is unprofitable," and "putting profits in command,". . . . They saw the question of whether or not to remove phenol (carried in waste water from the plant which damaged crops) as a question of "for whom?"[5]

This last question of "for whom?" may not sound very radical but it stands in opposition to the whole notion of efficiency in capitalist societies and those socialist ones which emulate them. This is not by way of denying the difficulty of answering that question, but the very insistence that this be the primary question of production represents a radical departure for the Chinese economy.

It is in this context that the Chinese have moved to deal with the problem of what they call the "three wastes" (waste gas, liquid, and solid residue), not as a technical problem or a marginal one but rather as fulfilling a primary goal of socialist society. This has, particularly in the last years, been a subject of mass campaigns with an extensive impact:

> The aim of socialist industrial production is not profits but the prosperity of the country and the peoples' happiness. The capitalist practice of only seeking profit while ignoring the harm done to the people by the "three wastes" is alien to socialism.
>
> We consider preventing the "three wastes" from harming the people and turning the harmful into the beneficial as an indispensable factor in industrial construction, from city planning, arranging and selecting factory sites to technological processes. A new industrial enterprise is not allowed to go into production if it lacks necessary measures to deal with the "three wastes" properly. Old enterprises which have not yet solved the problem of the "three wastes" are actively working on it.[6]

The Chinese model has not rejected growth but has spread industry throughout the country rather than intensifying urbanization. In the process, great emphasis has been put on having industry and agriculture serve each other, rather than allowing the former to destroy the latter with its wastes. There has been an incessant campaign in China to make the cities and their surrounding suburban areas as self-sufficient in food as possible. This is accomplished by city workers volunteering in farm work and using waste products of industry in surrounding agriculture. There are many reports in the Chinese press of such practice but a few samples will do for illustration here.

The city of Shenyang is a large, heavily industrialized city in Northeast China which has a population of several million with 60 percent in the urban area and the rest in surrounding suburbs. In the past, grain and vegetables from seventeen provinces were transported over a long distance to feed Shenyang's population. To cut down on this wasted transportation, to narrow the gap between country and city, and to foster self-reliance, there was a mass mobilization typical to the Chinese economy:

> During the busy farming seasons, such as spring ploughing, summer hoeing, and autumn harvesting and planting, both the city and its surrounding villages were mobilized, and army men and civilians all took part in farm work. The number of people from the city participating in this work last year was more than three million. In preparing for ploughing last year, the city sent more than 500,000 people to help with the accumulation and transportation of fertilizer in the countryside.

To support the villages, Shenyang workers in the last two years used waste and old materials to repair and make more than 1,100 sets of equipment for electrically operated wells and large quantities of other farm machinery. Many industrial and mining enterprises went in for multi-purpose use of materials and produced insecticides and chemical fertilizer to aid agriculture.[7]

As a result of these efforts, according to the *Peking Review,* "Shenyang is now basically self-sufficient in food, grain and vegetables."[8]

Another account tells of the massive project that built a 30-kilometer-long drainage conduit which takes 300,000 tons of waste water from Shanghai daily to irrigate the surrounding farmland.[9] Still another tells of the Peking Winery which uses its "three wastes" to produce hydrogen, chlorine gas, helium, polycrystalline silicon, adenosine triphosphate, 4-24 bacterial insecticide, and a plant hormone.[10] And a commune on the outskirts of Peking now, with improved irrigation, provides one-seventh of Peking's vegetable supply cutting out previous long-distance food transports.[11]

The use of urban sewage for agricultural watering and fertilization is well advanced over the practice in most modern countries. It is startling in comparison to free-world cities like Seoul which haven't even developed a basic sewage system. The city of Changchun in northern China, for example, built a 10-kilometer-long canal which brings:

52,000 tons of sewage water from the city's factories and living quarters [to] drain off and irrigate 330 hec-

tares of paddy fields and 1,200 hectares of other crop-
land. The people's communes, using sewage water
which contains nitrogen and phosphorous to irrigate
their farmland, save a total of about 3,500 tons of
chemical fertilizer a year. The project also creates
conditions for multiple use of sewer water.[12]

Orville Schell, who combines his academic interests
in China and the environment with being a water
commissioner in Bolinas, California, concluded in his
study:

> While the U.S. is still installing primary or secondary
> treatment plants for sewage (namely, partially treat-
> ing sewage, adding chlorine and getting rid of it), the
> Chinese are moving towards ecologically sound and
> financially rewarding tertiary treatment plants which
> seek to re-use both water and solids, thereby disposing
> of nothing simply for the sake of disposal.[13]

The Chinese spend far less time talking about the
"environment" than we in the U.S. do, for they do
not see it as a special or abstract problem. It is rather,
for them, a question of getting the fullest "use value"
from human productivity as a whole rather than
specialized profit.

There is a basic optimism to this dialectical view
and it comes from putting humans at the center of
history and ascribing to them the power to comprehend and transform objective reality. It is a spirit
summed up best in one of the Cultural Revolution's
"three constantly read articles": the fable of The Old
Man Who Moved the Mountain. This story, of a man
who could contemplate literally moving a mountain

bit by bit from the front of his door, has in fact become a watchword of economic activity within China. There are frequent reports of mountains leveled, of deserts planted with trees, and of rivers tamed, all based on the example of that fable.

For this reason the Chinese do not see population as the source of the world's problems. In June of 1972 in Stockholm, at the first United Nations Conference on the Human Environment, the Chinese delegation stated:

> Here we would like to deal briefly with the relationship between population growth and protection of the human environment. We hold that of all things in the world, people are the most precious. The masses have boundless creative power. To develop social production and create social wealth depends on people, and to improve the human environment also depends on people.[14]

The delegation pointed to the fact that China had experienced population growth from five hundred million in 1949 to seven hundred million in 1970, but "because we had ... overthrown the system of exploitation, the standard of living of the people has not lowered but gradually improved in spite of the relatively rapid growth of the population."[15]

This is a telling argument, for the Chinese are taking care of their own people using a very small proportion of world-resource consumption. The Chinese have quite rightly interpreted the concern with population to very often be an attack on the right of

246 America After Nixon

the poor and populous to develop, and they noted this at Stockholm:

> We support the developing countries in building their national economies on the principle of independence, exploiting their natural resources in accordance with their own needs and gradually improving the well-being of their people. Each country has the right to determine its own environmental standards and policies in the light of its own conditions, and no country whatsoever should undermine the interests of the developing countries under the pretext of protecting the environment.[16]

The opposite view has been expressed by Dr. Paul Ehrlich, author of the bestseller, *The Population Bomb*. He maintained that the underdeveloped countries were like sick patients crowding into a medical tent and that the rich countries were the doctors who could not serve all. *This was asserted despite the fact that the declining rate of population growth in the United States has not in any noticeable way cut into its accelerating use of resources.*

Ehrlich's thesis had first been advanced in a book by William and Paul Paddock called *Famine Nineteen Seventy-Five!* which called for the food-rich countries (particularly the United States) to make basic political decisions for the poor before dispensing their grain. As Ehrlich said:

> Perhaps we should have supported Katanga, not the Congo. Perhaps we should now support Biafra, not Nigeria. West Pakistan might receive aid but not East Pakistan. It might be to our advantage to have

some UDC's [underdeveloped countries] more divided or even rearranged, especially along economic axes.[17]

He is in favor of unilateral United States action toward these goals, as in the case of applying pressure on India to sterilize all Indian males with three or more children. "Coercion? Perhaps, but coercion in a good cause."[18]

To Ehrlich there is really only the problem of population. All others are results of that one, and therefore the only "politics" that he is concerned with are those of population control. So one of his heroes at the time was Khan of Pakistan.

The Paddocks think that Pakistan, at least West Pakistan may be such a country. Others to whom I have spoken agree. Our food aid may give the Pakistani government, under the tough-minded leadership of President Ayub Khan, time to press home its population control and agricultural development programs.[19]

Such apolitical tough-minded talk is really a cover for cultural chauvinism and racism. It is also uninformed. Ayub Khan was hardly a tough-minded leader, despite his birth-control position, for there are other basic issues; and, as the Bangladesh fiasco demonstrated, some of his policies were disastrous.

Needless to say, Ehrlich views any criticism of imperialism's role in Katanga or Pakistan as extraneous quibbling. Indeed, he is in favor of a consortium of the world's powerful nations making the basic political decisions for the have-nots:

> My suggestion would be that the United States, Russia, Great Britain, Canada, Japan, Australia, Europe and other DC's [developed countries] immediately set up, through the United Nations, a machinery for "area rehabilitation." This plan would involve simultaneous population control, agricultural development, and, where resources warrant it, industrialization of selected countries. The bedrock of this program would be population control, necessarily including migration control to prevent swamping of aided areas by the less fortunate.[20]

The idea that the superpowers could disinterestedly make the basic socioeconomic decisions in the best interests of the world's population is a convenient view. If the problem is simply one of population, the real villains are not U.S. industrialists, Russian chauvinists, advertising agencies, CIA agents, etc., but the Third World people who refuse to follow Ehrlich's prescriptions. Not only does Ehrlich ignore imperialist penetration but, on the contrary, his plan for saving the world is based on extending the current Third World marketing offensive by the multinational advertising agencies:

> Possibly the first step in all areas would be to set up relay stations and distribute small transistorized T.V. sets to villages for communal viewing of satellite-transmitted programs. We must have channels for reaching the largely rural populations of the "other world." T.V. programs would explain the rehabilitation plan for each area. These programs would have to be produced with the combined skill of Madison Avenue, of people with great expertise in the subjects to be presented, and of people with intimate knowledge of the target population. The programs could

be presented both "straight" and as cleverly devised "entertainment."[21]

In case the natives fail to respond to the bead game or "entertainment approach," the TV channel could be used to notify them of Ehrlich's final solution that food supplies would be cut off if they failed to cooperate.

What the Chinese communists have demonstrated is that the question of population and food supply is a political one; and that it can be viewed as a matter of the way human beings conduct themselves in relation to the land rather than a matter of mechanical input. So it is really the Ehrlichs and not the "ChiComs" who have the view of man as robot. The Maoist answer to the dark Malthusian numbers game is that such pessimism stems from a contempt for the masses of people who inhabit the earth:

> Ideas of stagnation, pessimism and inertia are all wrong. On the question of the human environment there is no ground for any negative view. We are convinced that along with social progress and the advance of science and technology, and provided that the governments of the countries concerned genuinely take the interests of the people to heart, take the coming generations to heart, rely on the masses and bring their role into full play, they will certainly be able to exploit and utilize natural resources more fully.[22]

Since Ehrlich did not undertake a serious examination of comparative social systems, he failed to come up with the obvious fact that a people's attitude toward the population problem is not unrelated to their general social outlook. In India, for example, the high birth rate is a response to economic insecurity; in China, collectivization breaks down the need for large families. It is also obvious that effective birth control must flow out of a people's understanding of its use and necessity. Forced birth control, short of sterilization of the kind Ehrlich recommends, simply doesn't work. In China the government has pursued an extensive and varied program of birth control which has started to pay off. It is viewed as a problem but not *the* problem. Despite an increase in China's population,

> The country has not become poorer but has gradually become prosperous, the people's living environment has not deteriorated but has gradually improved. Of course this in no way means that we approve of the unchecked growth of population. Our government has always advocated family planning, and the publicity, education and other necessary measures adopted over the years have begun to produce some effects. It is wholly groundless to think that population growth in itself will bring about pollution and damage of the environment and give rise to poverty and backwardness.[23]

Western writers and development experts have based their gloomy prognostications about populations on a simple mathematical extrapolation which takes little cognizance of social and economic forces at work in the Third World. But it is illogical to simply project population growth on the basis of current conditions, assume an exponential growth, and divide a constant land mass into that projection. Changing social systems not only have an effect on population policies but also on the efficient use of land and indeed on the reclamation of new land, all of which has been demonstrated in China.

Indeed, the central problem in the world currently is not one of too many people per acre of arable land, but of insufficient utilization of the labor force of the Third World. The problem of massive unemployment and underemployment is more pressing than that of famine. Whereas in China socialist planning has permitted a maximum use of the labor force by bringing industrialization to the countryside, in the "free-world countries" the opposite movement of people to the big cities to serve the needs of capitalist entrepreneurs has brought disaster. As the conservative *Far Eastern Economic Review* reported:

> . . . the underdeveloped world faces an "employment problem" well before any spectre of imminent general starvation has appeared. The rapidly swelling cities (Tehran, Calcutta, Jakarta, Manila) increasingly swarm with hundreds of thousands—even millions—of unemployed or barely employed. Why? The answers are not yet clear; the land seems technically capable of giving actual nutrition to many more millions of households than it seems socially able to employ . . .[24]

The problem is caused by social dislocation on both ends. Industrial investment is anarchistic in its impact, and agricultural improvements such as the U.S.-sponsored green revolution have forced peasants off the land without giving them alternative work:

> ... concern has also been expressed over the methods by which the green revolution has been introduced. For example, in the Punjab increased demand for irrigation and fertilizer have been met by a concentration of former tenant holdings into the hands of landowners who, by using tractors, dispense with the labour of the large majority of those who used to work the land.[25]

These people then do not receive any blessings from the green revolution but are, on the contrary, forced to migrate to the slums of the big cities. The International Labor Organization estimated in 1970 that by 1980, three hundred million new jobs outside of agriculture would be needed in the Third World. In order to avoid urbanization, a new rural social unit like the Chinese commune must materialize, allowing for collective ownership of the land and therefore collective benefits from new agricultural technology. This would further allow for the planned utilization of agricultural labor in industrial projects in the countryside.

In the capitalist model, employment depends upon the individual decisions of capitalists bent on profit and not overall social need. In the Third World countries, development by the multinationals has led to the proliferation of large modern industries, divorced from the local economies and hence at the mercy of the export trade and the whims of the rich nations. Thus the unemployment problem of the Third World is pitted against the unemployment problem of the rich nations:

> No one who remembers the imposition of quotas on textile imports by U.S. President Richard Nixon (or the earlier, though less publicized, quotas imposed by the United Kingdom) can fail to be aware of the political obstacles awaiting a further pursuit of this policy for industrialization. If raising employment in the underdeveloped world by this method means sharply aggravating employment problems of the advanced nations, then its application will be shortlived indeed.[26]

The multinationals are concerned with "quality" production for the world market which they associate with complex machinery and production processes. The cruder production of a commune plant might indeed depart from their standard. At the same time it would be less wasteful of resources and in particular the human one of unemployed rural labor. But more importantly, here we get back to the questions of how basic decisions are made and for whom. It is possible to have very elaborate arguments about the content of freedom in China, but we do know that large numbers of ordinary people living on communes and working in factories have a great deal of input into questions of how and what to produce. Decisions are made quite differently for the people of the Third World, and I will leave it to the *Far Eastern Economic Review,* a Dow-Jones publication, to summarize that process:

254 America After Nixon

> Most important of all have been the practices of the credit institutions. In underdeveloped countries, capital is scarce and industrial entrepreneur style is usually recent, so there is typically great dependence on banks in the financing of both private and public industrial projects.

> But bankers naturally favour capital-intensive techniques which yield them a reassuring fixed asset collateral; they also prefer to save themselves time and trouble by concentrating their loanable funds in (say) a few score large projects rather than attempting to spread them out in a multitude of smaller labour-intensive factories.[27]

It is this sort of decision-making which is really at the heart of the problem of waste, poverty, and development in the Third World. The mixture of a few large industries with sweatshops brings unemployment and social dislocation. Conservation of resources in the Third World must start not with sterilizing people or even simply stopping population growth, but rather with the effective utilization of the existing population which can only come about by their having power collectively over their environment, and hence a real stake in development. To dwell on curtailing growth of population and/or resources, and to ignore these power realities, is simpleminded. As the Chinese said at the United Nations Conference on the Human Environment at Stockholm:

> In our opinion, the increasingly serious pollution and damage of the human environment in certain regions, which has become an outstanding issue, is

mainly the result of the development of capitalism
into imperialism . . .[28]

In answer to the alarmists, the Chinese said that
decent ways of organizing human society exist:

> . . . this problem can be solved along with social
> progress and the advance of science and technology.
> We must not give up eating for fear of choking, nor
> refrain from building our own industry for fear of
> pollution and damage to the environment.[29]

The Chinese have earned the right to make that
statement by their example of a social organization
which is one of the least wasteful in the world. They
have shown an immense ability to free themselves
from the restraints of nature without destroying it.

There is simply no way to logically separate this
question of frugality from the method of decision-
making, nor to compare China with our own society
(or increasingly Russia's) on the question of private
profit-making.

But to accent Mao's line provides only the basis for
dealing with the problem and not the solution. For
example, even though Mao's dictum, "Taking agriculture as the foundation, and industry as the leading
sector," may be taken to heart, it still doesn't answer
basic questions of what to produce. These have to be
"struggled out" continuously as the following inci-
dent in China's *Economic Reporter* attests:

> "Does it pay to turn out simple screws for water-
> wheels that sell for one and a half cents each?"

This question aroused a heated discussion in a machine building plant of East China's Kiangsu Province. In fact, it boiled down to the issue of how industry should support agriculture.

Some people thought that since screws give little profit, the plant should concentrate on producing farm machines that sell for a big sum. This idea was criticized during the discussion, because production of that type of screws involves a major issue of giving support to agriculture.[30]

It is only by paying attention to this intricate interweaving of decision-making in China between rural and urban and the national and local economies, that one can begin to talk seriously about the population problem of that country or any other facet of its development. For in all of these matters the Chinese proceed as a people from such a fundamentally different mode of behavior than our own, that to predict disaster for them, based on the assumptions of our own society, is pointless. The difference is a matter of "political consciousness." We may believe that history is accidental or something shaped by a few gifted or audacious heroes, but the Chinese seem to be quite addicted to the notion that ordinary people can make history and that they can do so in a way beneficial to their own best interests. They are in some ways the most naive or optimistic of democrats, and to understand their "obstinacy" on the population question we have to comprehend their humanism. This was revealed in the most recent official statement I could find on Chinese population policy which appeared in the *Peking Review* of December 7, 1973:

> Of all things in the world, people are the most precious. Once the people become masters of their own destiny, every miracle can be performed. As working people, human beings are first of all producers and then consumers . . .
>
> China pursues a policy of developing its national economy in a planned way, including the policy of planned population growth. We do not approve of anarchy either in material production or in human reproduction.
>
> Man should control himself as well as nature. In order to realize planned population growth, what we are doing is, on the basis of energetically developing production and improving the people's living standards, to develop medical and health services throughout the rural and urban areas and strengthen our work in maternity and child-care, so as to reduce the mortality rate on the one hand and regulate the birth rate by birth planning on the other.
>
> What we mean by birth planning is not just practicing birth control, but taking different measures in the light of different circumstances. In densely populated areas where the birth rate is high, marriage at later age and birth control are advocated. However, active medical treatment is provided for those suffering from sterility.[31]

I find in that last sentence, whatever its apparent contradictions, more real concern for human welfare than in most of the writings of the zero-population people or the proponents of the free-world growth models.

part four

BEYOND NIXON: THE WASTE ECONOMIES AND THE CRISIS OF CONTROL

chapter 13

DUBIOUS DÉTENTE

While it is no doubt true, as Lenin argued, that imperialism is the highest stage of capitalism it is equally true that consumerism is the highest stage of imperialism. Lenin wrote before the full flowering of advertising, packaging, brand-name marketing, and all of the other refinements of the culture of capitalism. Cultural imperialism, with its superstructure of product fantasy, media co-option, and neo-religious materialism is far more pervasive and seductive than either Marx or Lenin could have imagined. Even in the Soviet Union, consumerism has turned out to be as destructive of socialist values as any of the factors Lenin had anticipated and viewed with alarm, such as the difficulty of ensuring democratic decision-making within the Party and the instability of Stalin's personality.

Indeed the former conflict between the Soviet Union's vision of socialism and Western capitalism's vision of democracy is fast becoming a grand international rat race for the biggest pile of garbage per person. Since the Soviet Union is still a distant second in the packaging business, the world culture for the next period will no doubt continue to be dominated by the American corporations. If the Soviets are ever to catch up they must follow the advice of some of their dissident writers and more exactly copy the institutions of American life. Which is all fun and games for everyone except the ordinary citizens of both countries who have to hustle to pay for all the things they have been conned into viewing as necessities. In addition they must carry the expenditures of their respective bureaucracies' acceleration of an expensive arms race. For the inhabitants of the poorer world, the words of the "Internationale," "arise ye prisoners of starvation," must seem as relevant as ever, but if they look to the Soviet Union for deliverance, all they will find are Kissinger-like references to the new era of peace and an injunction to stand still and allow their resources to flow unhindered by revolutionary outbursts which might disturb the peaceful détente of the giants.

But powerful historical forces cannot be locked into a timeframe to suit the needs of leaders who are at the moment powerful. Both the Western capitalist world and the Soviet Union, in the management of their own peoples and economies, are experiencing profound difficulties which keep bubbling up to the surface, unraveling carefully worked out arrangements to preserve the status quo. No longer mesmerized by the official dreams, the citizens of the waste societies are increasingly reluctant to perform the taxing rituals of ambition and acquisition. For the poor in both worlds there is a new sense of power mingled with desperation that can no longer simply be co-opted or easily bought off. Neither the delusions of American democracy nor Soviet socialism are sufficient to keep in check the yearnings of multitudes for a significant measure of social justice. An insistence that life on this earth be more charitable, rational, and rewarding now cuts across the lines of official ideologies.

Perhaps the most important declaration of independence from great power politics occurred at the extraordinary conference of the UN General Assembly, which was convened in April 1974, at the instigation of the Algerian government. It came in the wake of the oil producers' boycott, which had shaken the economies of the major powers but had also played havoc with those of the poor. As the most progressive of the oil producers, it was Algeria's aim to put that boycott into the larger perspective of a world resource crisis. The conference revealed a new level of unity among the poorer countries on the key issues of an emerging world politic. In no uncertain terms a "new world order" was demanded.

The dominant tone was set in the opening address by Algeria's President Houari Boumediene, who explicitly denied the assumption that the great powers' détente was sufficient for a solution of the world's problems.

> We cannot fail to note that the gradual shift out of the Cold War context has not been accompanied by a corresponding improvement in the condition of the countries of the Third World.
>
> On the contrary, tension and war have been transferred to Asia, Africa, and Latin America which have become the zones where all the contradictions of our contemporary world are concentrated and exacerbated.[1]

With the passing of the central tension between the U.S. and Russia, a more profound struggle was at last surfacing: "The central question is the opposition between the needs of the poor countries and those of the rich countries."[2]

This theme was amplified by the Chinese delegation to the conference, which noted, that this special assembly of the UN marked a turning point in the line-up of the world's nations and in the role of the UN itself, which was passing from being a puppet of the U.S. to a forum expressing the needs of the world's people:

> This is the first time in the 29 years since the founding of the United Nations that a session is held specially to discuss the important question of opposing imperialist exploitation and plunder and effecting a change in international economic relations. This reflects that profound changes have taken place in the international situation.[3]

The Chinese argued that the Western imperialist bloc was disintegrating because of capitalist rivalries and that the socialist camp was "no longer in existence" because the Soviet Union had become social-imperialistic. This last term derives from Lenin's denigration of earlier socialist leaders who at the time of World War I, despite an internationalist rhetoric, blindly supported their national governments' expansionist policies. To the Chinese, the new world scene is made up of three worlds that are both interconnected and in contradiction to one another:

> The United States and the Soviet Union make up the First World. The developing countries in Asia, Africa, Latin America and other regions make up the Third

World. The developed countries between the two
make up the Second World.[4]

The Chinese rejection of the "détente" is based on
the notion that it aims at establishing new spheres of
hegemony for the superpowers at the expense of the
Third World:

> Every day, they talk about disarmament but are
> actually engaged in arms expansion. Every day they
> talk about "détente" but are actually creating ten-
> sion. Wherever they contend, turbulence occurs. So
> long as imperialism and social-imperialism exist,
> there definitely will be no tranquility in the world,
> nor will there be "lasting peace." Either they will
> fight each other, or the people will rise in revolu-
> tion.[5]

Since the focus of this book is on America's role in
the world, I will have to avoid a more serious evalua-
tion of the Sino-Soviet dispute or the question of social imperialism. But there are several points to the
Chinese critique that do bear directly on our discussion. The first is that there definitely are, as previous
chapters have shown, at least two if not three worlds
and that most of the people of the world share a common oppression by what I have been calling the waste
economies. In this sense, China is definitely in the
Third World and the Soviet Union is not. Secondly,
given the meager access of the poorer countries to
raw materials and capital necessary for development,
the emphasis of the Soviet Union on consumerism,
space technology, the military, and other forms of
waste stands in contradiction to the needs of the

world's people. It is also obviously true that there cannot be a just détente which accepts a status quo of world poverty. As the Algerian president stated:

> Our century can no longer tolerate individual incomes less than a third of a dollar a day in 1974 or, as the expected results of the second development decade would seem to indicate, incomes barely equal to half a dollar in 1980.[6]

But the détente involves precisely such an acceptance, for its purpose is to cool out any turbulence which would threaten existing power relations. It is important to remember that the spirit of détente in no way made it difficult for the U.S. to engineer the overthrow of the Allende government in Chile, nor to establish a new alliance with corrupt Arab governments at the expense of the Palestinian people. For the Soviet Union to participate in this détente has meant at best acceptance of the U.S. initiative and at worst participation in the plunder.

In his speech to the Third World conference, the Chinese delegate offered some refreshing advice on the proper care and handling of superpowers, which may inhibit future generations of leftists from blindly attempting to apologize for foreign models, including the Chinese one:

> A superpower is an imperialist country which everywhere subjects other countries to its aggression, interference, control, subversion or plunder and strives for world hegemony. If capitalism is restored in a big socialist country, it will inevitably become a superpower. The Great Proletarian Cultural Revolution,

which has been carried out in China in recent years, and the campaign of criticising Lin Piao and Confucius now under way throughout China, are both aimed at preventing capitalist restoration and ensuring that socialist China will never change her colour and will always stand by the oppressed peoples and oppressed nations. If one day China should change her colour and turn into a superpower, if she too should play the tyrant in the world, and everywhere subject others to her bullying, aggression and exploitation, the people of the world should identify her social-imperialism, expose it, oppose it and work together with the Chinese people to overthrow it.[7]

Meanwhile our own government remains the most powerful force in most of the world. The collusion between the U.S. and Soviet governments has simply strengthened the hand of the American corporations. As the world is once again redivided into spheres of influence, the multinationals are retaining the choice franchises, as witnessed by the failure of Soviet policy in Latin America and the Mideast. The corporations favor the détente for they read into it assurances that the Soviets will use their influence to curtail the activity of local leftist forces. But it is an ultimately forlorn hope for the forces of radicalism now in the world are neither Soviet-inspired nor under their control or influence. The desires of the "haves" for normalization was echoed at the UN conference by Soviet Foreign Minister Andrei Gromyko, who, according to the UN press release, said: ". . . the turn towards détente and the amelioration of the international political climate had created a favorable environment for normalizing economic relations."[8]

But a more strident voice was heard from most Third World countries. In his opening speech Boumediene launched an attack on the power and role of the multinational corporations:

> Under the sole heading of profits declared by corporations, the capital that flowed out of the developing countries during the second half of the 1960–1970 development decade amounted to 23 billion dollars, which is one and one-half times total foreign aid proper (i.e. the grants) that the countries to which these companies belong made available to the developing countries.[9]

He went on to offer the case of Chile as an example of the political power of the corporations and as an illustration of why the Third World would inevitably be in conflict with their power:

> Chile has been the tragic scene of an imperialist plot fostered by the multinational corporations, leading to the destruction of the democratic institutions of that country and the heinous murder of President Salvador Allende, who had given the world an example of devotion and self-sacrifice . . .[10]

Like Castro a decade earlier, Allende had placed his country on the front line against the encroachments of the multinationals. However, it was not Allende's special fight as Boumediene saw it, but a struggle that had to be waged throughout the Third World:

> It must be recognized first of all that in the world in which we live all the strings of the world economy

are in the hands of a minority composed of the highly developed countries.

The will to gain and cling to their position of dominance over world resources has been the guiding principle in the behavior of the major imperialist powers of the world.[11]

Boumediene pointed out that this dominance has been exercised through varying mechanisms allowing the powerful to adjust to or co-opt sentiments for self-determination.

In fact, the colonial and imperialist powers accepted the principle of the right of peoples to self-determination only when they had already succeeded in setting up the institutions and the machinery that would perpetuate the system of pillage established in the colonial era.[12]

In the current era it is the multinational corporations that form that machinery, and it was Algeria's position—and one echoed by many others—that the nationalization of these corporations' foreign assets was a *prerequisite* for economic development. To recover control over their sovereignty the Third World countries would be inevitably pitted against the multinationals:

It is essential, therefore, that we should not lose sight of the fact that the effort to bring the task of recovery to fruition will remain without effect so long as international monopolies and multinational corporations, those past masters at the art of making concessions in order to safeguard the essentials, continue to control the multiple mechanisms whereby the wealth of the poor countries is transferred away from them, and mainly the system of pricefixing for raw materials.[13]

A major study for UNCTAD (the United Nations Conference on Trade and Development) concluded that the striking increases in commodity prices in the seventies had just managed to restore the terms of trade between primary commodities and manufactured goods to the level they had occupied in 1950. "The average terms of trade (volume of manufactures that could be purchased by a given basket of primary commodities) had declined steadily throughout the 1950s and 1960s."[14]

The Secretary General of UNCTAD pointed out that:

> . . . the main beneficiaries of the commodity boom had been the developed countries themselves. The increase in export earnings attributable to primary products other than petroleum was $29 billion in 1973—nearly three times greater than the corresponding increase of $11 billion in the commodity exports of the developing countries.[15]

He went on to observe that "The activities of multinational corporations would have to be harnessed and made consistent with the development objectives of developing countries."[16]

The working paper that formed the basis of unity among the Third World nations participating in the conference went even further in its demands than the Secretary General. In calling for the "Establishment of a New International Economic Order," it stated that an attack on the power of the multinationals or transnationals was the first step toward such a new order:

> . . . every country has the right to exercise effective control over its natural resources and their exploitation with means suitable to its own situation, including the right of nationalization or transfer of ownership to its nationals;

> . . . nationalization is an expression of the sovereign right of every country to safeguard its resources; in this connection, every country has the right to fix the amount of possible compensation and mode of payment, while possible disputes have to be solved in accordance with the domestic laws of every country.[17]

The particular use of loan funds as a weapon for protecting the interests of the multinationals was criticized at this conference as it was in the same month at the annual meeting of the InterAmerican Development Bank which took place in Santiago, Chile. There Venezuela and Peru led the fight against the U.S. government's possession of a veto power over loans. This veto power had been used as a weapon against Allende's Chile when it had begun nationalization of foreign companies. As *The New York Times* reported:

> Guillermo Marco del Pont, the Peruvian Finance Minister asserted that "powerful lobbies" representing multinational corporations had tried to "restrict and condition the free use of the bank's resources"

when disagreements arose between the United States and the Latin-American countries over expropriations.[18]

At Santiago the U.S. position was stated by George Shultz, then Secretary of the Treasury, in a style which was a good bit more blunt than the careful diplomatic language used by Kissinger at the UN conference. As Kissinger had put it, "the global economy requires a trade, monetary and investment system that sustains industrial civilization and stimulates its growth."[19] Shultz, however, got right to the point: ". . . if we cannot feel secure from expropriation, and certainly from expropriation without just compensation, you will not have a flow of capital—private or public."[20]

Just why public funds should be tied to the compensation of private U.S. corporations has never in recent times been the subject of serious political debate in this country—it is simply one of the givens of our politics. It is once again a reflection of that absurdity that the average American tax-paying assembly-line worker for a multinational corporation is expected to have the same foreign policy interests as the owners of that corporation. But when Shultz resigned his cabinet position shortly after the Santiago meeting, he was to become a vice-president of the Bechtel Corporation. He was leaving government service for a corporate life that was very familiar to him. As *Business Week* reported: "Stephen D. Bechtel, Jr. last week hired one of his golfing buddies to handle 'special tasks and assignments' for him at the family's Bechtel Corporation."[21]

This family firm has 40 billion dollars worth of construction contracts and has operated in ninety-one countries and on all continents.[22] It is a prototype of the multinational:

> One thing is certain: The hiring of Shultz underscores the growing importance of political and financial expertise to big engineering outfits that operate on a global scale. Roughly half of San Francisco-based Bechtel's work is overseas, much of it in resource development projects for developing countries.[23]

Who was Shultz representing at that conference in Chile—the taxpayers or the interests of multinational companies? And can you do both? These are basic questions because American citizens are increasingly being represented by their government as standing in opposition to rising Third World forces and on the side of the multinationals. There is, however, no hard evidence to support the assertion of the multinationals that their operations improve the standard of living of the average American either through lower raw-material prices or jobs.

On the contrary, the overwhelming evidence suggests that these operations are as bad a bargain for the U.S. economy generally as they are good for the multinationals. It is their high-handed practices which have now forced some Third World commodity producers to band together to raise prices, which the multina-

276 America After Nixon

tionals have now passed on to consumers. Since their oligopolistic regulation of the flow of resources and prices is aimed at profit maximization, it must be assumed that a loosening of their grip and the emergence of a more competitive market would be to the benefit rather than the detriment of the average American consumer.

If the price of manufactured goods were not maintained at an artificially high level by the oligopolists then the world-wide demand for them would increase and presumably also the number of American jobs. This would also be true if American manufacturers were not permitted to establish runaway factories in foreign lands, thereby undermining the domestic wage rate. To assume that these corporations are in the best position to make decisions for American consumers and workers is a denial of fundamental political freedoms. It only makes sense if one assumes that the freedom of the American consumer is inherently bound up with the perpetuation of the life-style and culture created by the corporations. If we must hunger for their trinkets in a spirit of fanaticism that transcends all other considerations then we are indeed dependent upon the wisdom of their resource allocation.

The dilemma that confronts the American citizen was raised pointedly at the Third World conference by many delegations. In defending the rise in oil prices Boumediene noted that this was hardly the major source of the world's grief:

> The impact of the price of oil in overall cost makeup has always been ridiculously small; it remains so today; thus, if we wish to throttle inflation, it is necessary to attack the most significant items of expenditure.
>
> In particular, it is necessary to eliminate the phenomenon of overconsumption and gadgetization and, more generally the waste, which runs rampant throughout the developed economies.
>
> The same holds true with respect to the expenditures engendered by the arms race and by military aggression and those dedicated to the various space programs.[24]

The connection between waste and the multinationals was stated forcefully by Emilio O. Rabasa, the Foreign Minister of Mexico. Since Rabasa represents a country that has in recent times been close to the U.S. and presumably benefited from "good" economic relations, I reprint his remarks at length as reported in the UN press release:

> Mr. Rabasa went on to say that the monopolistic countries were digging their own graves and that the insolent opulence of today would be converted into the humble poverty of tomorrow unless they understood that it was in their own interest to alleviate the situation in the developing countries.
>
> Referring to the enormous influence in the field of trade and production exercised by multinational corporations, Mr. Rabasa said that, according to various estimates, *by 1985, 80 per cent of the industry of the countries with a market economy would be controlled by 300 to 400 such corporations.*
>
> The figures, which were revealing and terrifying, he went on, indicated that the petroleum industry was

in the hands of six companies, that the petrochemical industry was dominated by 15 firms, the electronics industry by 10, the production of tires by eight, the production of glass by five and the production of paper by nine.

To make matters worse, he stated, when their insatiable appetite for profit was not satisfied, they violated by means of political pressure the principles of nonintervention and self-determination.[25]

And it is this insatiable appetite which they have implanted in us since birth. Overconsumption on the part of citizens of the developed countries is no more a real expression of individual desires and needs than it is for a Third World consumer of the same items. More importantly it also represents the limits of choice deriving from the culture of monopoly capitalism. If the oligopolistic market is the essential arena for decision-making about resource allocation, then more social patterns of consumption will go by the board. (We can have a hundred back yards, each with its own set of swings, or a community playground.) Such a method of decision-making is a dangerous anachronism in a world which cries out for a high degree of integrated and world-wide planning as a precondition to that "New International Economic Order."

If the current business-as-usual is a disaster course then it is in the interest of most of the world's population and most definitely the vast majority of those in the developed countries to get off that course. But one does not set about building a new economic order by continuing to rely on the prime units of the old, which in this case would be the multinationals.

Current American foreign policy has transferred the initiative to the multinationals at the moment when they must be replaced. The only other vital machinery of our foreign policy appears to lie in the military arena, which continues to expand in grand indifference to the various diplomatic peace offensives and other moves to establish détente. This area of our policy is not only the most obvious source of waste but also stands as an obstacle to the spending of public funds for the use of Third World and domestic social development.

While Henry Kissinger was streaking around the world building his structures of peace, his counterpart in the defense department was making plans that appeared to be based on the assumption that the Cold War was just beginning. In presenting his whopping 1975 budget to Congress, Defense Secretary James R. Schlesinger acknowledged the strangeness of his request: "A policy requiring us to maintain our military strength and alliances while we are actively pursuing détente with the Soviet Union and the Peoples' Republic of China may appear to some as incongruous."[26]

Again it is as if nothing has really changed. We are still to live in the fear of nuclear destruction no matter how many toasts to peace our diplomats drink. The key element in the new defense budget is the accelerated development of even more sophisticated nuclear weapons and missile systems. Describing what has come to be known within the administration as a strategy of "Mutual Assured Destruction," Schlesinger's report to Congress stated:

> Even after a more brilliantly executed and devastating attack than we believe our potential adversaries could deliver, the United States would retain the capability to kill more than 30 per cent of the Soviet population and destroy more than 75 per cent of Soviet industry. At the same time we could hold in reserve a major capability against the PRC [Peoples' Republic of China].[27]

This would suggest that either we do not take the détente seriously and that the superpowers are very much still scrambling for world hegemony or that the military budget is an important prop to the domestic economy and therefore needs to be somehow justified. It would appear to be both.

The détente is in that sense artificial because it is not based on an end to the spoils system or a real commitment to a fundamental solution to the world's grave economic problems. As such it can never be better than a holding action for the convenience of the powerful. But it would also be unwise to de-emphasize the economic importance of the military budget, particularly to those corporations which make up what used to be called the military-industrial complex and which are still very much in business.

The end of the major U.S. involvement in Vietnam has not brought about that much-longed-for conversion of guns to butter. The Nixon strategy instead was to further impoverish domestic social programs

and foreign economic assistance while increasing
military spending. Despite the argument of some
reformers that socially useful programs could be as
profitable to the large corporations as military ones,
it does not seem that the corporations themselves believe it. Faced with the largest military budget in U.S.
history, with the exception of the World War II year
of 1942, it is obvious that such spending is a response
less to the fluctuations of international politics and
more to such constants as corporate profit-making.
Nor has the U.S. economy yet demonstrated in the
post-Depression years that it is viable without the
infusion of large-scale military expenditures.

A study of the military budget by the Brookings
Institute predicts that military expenditures will
reach a level of $142 billion by 1980 with an average
increase of 5.2 percent a year in *real* spending. The
Brookings study concluded with the accurate but
shocking observation that if these projections hold,
"there would be no room for a shift in federal spending from military to civilian purposes."[28]

What this means then is a perpetuation of a conflict between financing for the solution of domestic
and world-wide socioeconomic problems, on the one
hand, and the demand for lower taxes and the curtailing of inflation, on the other. It cheats the taxpayer
of the logical fruits of détente which should be the
elimination of the military spending that now has
added up to over $1.5 trillion in the postwar period.
That the interest of the average American lies in a
dismantling of this cozy military-corporate relation-

ship should be clear, but no serious political force has yet emerged which could tap this sentiment. Mr. Nixon's successor, Gerald Ford, and his potential opponent Scoop Jackson are both known to be even more committed than Nixon to the military prerogative. The mounting of a massive political alternative to the corporate-military hierarchy is the most significant item for the American agenda and long overdue. It is inexcusable that ordinary Americans should continue to be led to believe that their needs for economic and physical security are in conflict with the compelling needs of the poor of this world (including the U.S. poor) for a decent standard of living. This profound aberration in our national thinking flows from the inane proposition that the large corporations and the various bureaucracies that service them form a necessary bridge between the world's peoples and are thus entitled to be the arbiters of our culture and politics. It is not merely a matter of common decency but of sheer survival to assert that foreign plunder is not the equivalent of security or freedom. Certainly with a receding of Cold War hysteria one would have expected a full-scale and outraged assault on that major pool of waste and inflation, military spending. The fact that this has still not happened and that indeed military spending is escalating, is a scandal of far greater proportions than Watergate and even clearer proof of corporate influence over our political parties.

chapter 14

AMERICA
AFTER
NIXON

Although Richard Nixon was able to preside over the initiation of a grand new strategy of American foreign policy, he failed miserably to build a new consensus of support. Despite public approval of the lessening of Cold War tension, there is a sense of bewilderment and suspicion about where the new global politics is headed. A host of problems long suppressed under the false Cold War consensus have come bursting to the fore, demanding responses that can no longer be stilled by references to the national security or the needs of the "defense budget." As the economy becomes more and more shaky, the public begins to explore new possibilities in politics. Increasingly they have come to see that the corporations and their top government allies are at the center of what ails the society, be it the destruction of forests, skyrocketing meat prices, or gas shortages. America has not seemed so democratic and alive in over twenty-five years.

The striking shift in public opinion about the large corporations was documented at a May 1974 meeting of the American Association for Public Opinion Research. The findings of these pollsters "whose firms take periodic samples of public opinion for some of the country's largest corporations," was summarized by *The Washington Post* in quite dramatic terms:

> Big American corporations wield too much power in society, are insensitive to most social responsibilities, and ought to be broken up into smaller business units.

> These are the views now of a majority of Americans whose opinions of the business world have taken a drastic downward turn in the past decade, a panel of pollsters agreed today.[1]

The same article quoted Thomas W. Benham of the Opinion Research Corporation as saying that "the anti-monopoly sentiment is so high that it already is producing pressure for a new round of public ownership of transportation and utility companies. It will spread in 15 or 20 years to other businesses not traditionally subjected to public regulation." Meanwhile 75 percent of the American public feels that "too much power is concentrated in a few large companies" and 53 percent believe "that many large corporations should be broken up for the good of the country."[2] According to the surveys of the Roper organization, "Big business leads the list of institutions which are criticized for having too much power."[3]

As an AFL-CIO report noted, only a relatively small number of corporate giants, and not the general public or even "business," are benefiting from the current setup:

> Although an estimated 25,000 foreign affiliates are controlled by about 3,500 U.S. corporations, the bulk of those foreign operations is highly concentrated among the corporate giants. Professor Peggy Musgrave of Northeastern University reports that, in 1966, "over 80 percent of taxable income which U.S. corporations received from foreign sources . . . went to 430 corporations with asset size in excess of $250 million.[4]

And again citing Professor Musgrave: "Foreign investment may enhance the private profitability of U.S. capital, but it is likely to reduce the real wage to U.S. labor as well as the Government's tax share in the profits."[5]

After noting that the world economic situation had changed dramatically in the 1960s, as reflected by the development of a new globalism of large scale multinational private investment, the AFL-CIO pointed to what it considered the main danger—*that the American public was being disenfranchised* from influencing or controlling those investments. The multinationals were able to move outside the control of American workers, for the new market situation was no longer based on the export of products manufactured here:

> Within the confines of U.S. national frontiers, the spread of large national corporations was met gradually by institutional responses, such as the growth of national trade unions, and by government regulations, standards and controls. In the case of multinational corporate operations, there is no common international culture or legal structure. There is hardly even an international framework for the rapid development of international social controls and regulations.[6]

In the sixties, with the new globalism of corporate operations, the power of American unions began to slip away. In the process, the marriage between the big-labor bureaucracy and multinational corporations began to disintegrate. As the union report stated:

"What may be a rational decision for a U.S.-based multi-national company may be harmful to the American economy."[7]

The labor unions are merely the most organized of the disenfranchised. For most Americans, including most American workers who are not in the big unions, what power they had slipped away a long time before, but disillusionment was held in abeyance by the stifling Cold War political climate.

Kissinger has continued to speak as if the disunity caused by the Vietnam War and Watergate were exceptional to those events, and the events themselves accidental and not likely to be repeated: "I realize that we can't put Watergate behind us. But I hope that we can treat it as a cancer that has been excised . . ."[8] But Watergate's legacy to the American public has been less the revelation of the fact that an American President got caught playing with corporate funds and electronic tapes, and more a growing understanding of how government works. Watergate occurred in an atmosphere of disaffection with government power that had been most sharply increased by Vietnam. But there had been many such examples of government irrationality and public impotence in other areas. Kissinger would have done well to check out the nemesis of the Nixon administration, Walter Hickel, who was forced out of his post as Secretary of the Interior. In 1971, this three-time Nixon campaigner wrote his book, *Who Owns America?* to sound the alarm about public loss of power and, in doing so, spoke for a very widespread mood:

> Theodore Roosevelt, the father of enlightened en-
> vironmental policy in this country, was the first Presi-
> dent to see this problem in its entirety. The problem,
> even in his time, had to do with the obligation of
> ownership, and the public's residual interest in *any*
> ownership . . .
>
> It is clearly time to reaffirm that "we" and not
> "them" are the new voices of America, and that "we"
> and not "them" really own America.[9]

As Secretary of the Interior he had come smack up
against the power of the large corporations on virtually every issue, and had been forced back to the
populism that had given Estes Kefauver his clarity
in an earlier period of confrontation with the companies. Such populism comes to be informed and
often radicalized by the recognition that the current
institutional setups exclude the public from the key
economic issues. These institutions surrender the
major areas of decision-making to the "nonpolitical"
process of the economic market place—a deceptive
way of leaving the government in the position of protecting the property and prerogatives of the corporations, and even ensuring their economic survival,
without demanding social obedience or responsibility
in their conduct. This double standard of "competitive capitalism" was summarized quite bitterly by
Hickel:

> The people who criticize government most, are the
> same people who always come back to government
> with their hand out for financial help. Meanwhile
> they say, "The poor should help themselves, but our

companies should be helped by the government because it's in the national interest." Bullshit![10]

Whatever the problems of dealing with such companies within the interior of the U.S., the question
of regulating their global practices is many times
more difficult, beginning with the fact that even the
American government is not privy, as the energy
crisis showed, to the facts of their operations. Writing
before that particular foul-up, the AFL-CIO predicted as much with their description of the new
global system:

> Multi-national companies attempt to use a systems
> approach to global production, distribution and sales,
> which are spread through plants, offices, warehouses,
> sales agencies and other facilities in as many as 40 or
> more countries. Such companies can and do juggle
> the production, distribution and sales of components
> and finished products across national boundaries and
> oceans, based on the decisions of the top executives
> for the companies' private advantage. They can and
> do transfer currencies across national boundaries,
> often beyond the reach of the central banks of na-
> tions.[11]

Those decisions—"beyond the reach"—are life-and-
death decisions for people throughout the world, including Americans. When Kissinger talks of a stable
world order, it is one in which the norms of this
disenfranchisement will be accepted. When he says,
"If we don't tear ourselves to pieces domestically, we
can build something that will last beyond this administration,"[12] he implies incorrectly that our do-

mestic arguments are irrelevant to our lives here as well as to the international order.

By dealing with the irritants in the international system (revolutionaries, angry nationalists, etc.) and gaining agreement among the major powers on a "world order" and "stability," it has been Kissinger's hope in the style of a Metternich and the Congress of Vienna to preserve a balance of nation-state power that leaves the outstanding economic questions to be resolved in the international market. But the problem is that the international market is unstable and the multinational corporations are not self-regulating or even compatible with these nation-states. There is a built-in instability to their operations. This was summarized by two British economists:

> . . . it is clear that the growth of the multinational corporations, by itself, tends to weaken nation states. Multinational corporations render ineffective many traditional policy instruments, the capacity to tax, to restrict credit, to plan investment, etc., because of their international flexibility. In addition, multinational corporations act as a vehicle for the intrusion of the policies of one country into another with the ultimate effect of lessening the power of both. These tendencies have long been recognized in dependent developing countries, but it is now also evident that the United States as a *nation-state,* is losing some of its "independence" as it attempts to cope with the tangled web woven by its international business.[13]

This last thought contains the basic contradiction of the post-neo-colonial strategy promoted by Nixon and pursued by Kissinger. For, while cutting back on

older mechanisms of international control which were
found to be inoperative or too costly, it has been
forced to rely for basic decision-making on units
which have supranational interests that can then
come into conflict, not only with American workers,
but with the people as a whole, including important
sectors of the business community.

The economic isolationism of John Connally spoke
for those other business interests within the Nixon administration, and their viewpoints have only temporarily been mollified. In the last chapter of his book
(on the Kissinger policies), Henry Brandon points to
this as one of the problems with the "balance of mutual
weakness":

> Connally's outlook was not isolationist, but a mixture
> of nationalism and protectionism. It troubled not
> only foreign governments but also American business
> corporations which are, with their multinational op-
> erations and vast holdings overseas, the last American
> globalists. His views were not typical but they never-
> theless reflected the views in the U.S. Treasury and
> of many in Congress. Mr. Nixon considers himself an
> expert in foreign policy, and so does Kissinger, but
> neither has a real understanding of overseas economic
> affairs. As a consequence, there has been an unfortu-
> nate lack of American leadership in this field.[14]

In actuality, leadership has been abandoned to the
new American corporate globalists who are free of
public restraint. At least this was the case until the
energy crisis when the break between their interests
and ours became obvious.

America after Nixon will now be continuously plagued by such conflicts of interest, which will cheat the Kissinger-Nixon vision of the domestic consensus needed to build what Kissinger hoped would be "something that will last beyond this administration." America will be plagued because the problems built into the new "structure of peace" will be Nixon's legacy to the nation. There will be no easy going back from that structure. The new administration cannot simply summon the return of the Cold War, no matter how desirable that might seem for ensuring domestic tranquility. It will have one of two choices —either to move to make America's presence in the international economy more responsive to the American and the world's people or to suppress the doubts and opposition of both. To succeed in the second, it would have to do Watergate dirty tricks on the grand level which some would call fascism.

The "new majority" in America is populist in its opposition to centralized power and its determination to restore citizen control over political life. It is a left-of-center majority. With the Cold War basis of his constituency obliterated, Nixon's main public appeal as President came as a result of dovish overtures to China and Russia, and not through the hard line on bombing Vietnam or law and order. Analysis of his 1972 "new majority" which defeated McGovern found that it never existed, if by "new" was meant "conservative." As reported in *The New York Times*:

Louis Harris, the pollster, is sure that the Nixon majority in 1972 was never the "new majority," as described. Mr. Nixon's strongest appeal, the Harris surveys found, was in foreign policy where the emphasis of Mr. Nixon's trip to China and détente with the Russians was change, not conservatism. On economics and the "social issue," including forced school busing, Mr. Nixon did not have majority approval at election time, Mr. Harris asserts.[15]

The inherent conflict of Nixon's administration was between this reasonable posture on the communists and the necessity to maintain an unquestioning climate of opinion in which to support conservative business and social policies. In the event that readers feel I may have overstated the new freedom to think politically brought about by the end of the Cold War, I would refer them to further findings of the Harris survey concerning those the American people considered enemies. Mark the shift in a mere six-year period. According to the *Times* account:

"In 1967," Mr. Harris observed in an interview, "substantial majorities of our sample—60 to 75 per cent —thought the following people were 'dangerous or harmful to the country': people who didn't believe in God, black militants, student demonstrators, prostitutes, homosexuals. In the fall of 1973 we couldn't find a majority to say that any one of those groups was dangerous."

"Today," he continued, "the people considered 'dangerous' by a majority of Americans are these: people who hire political spies (52 per cent); generals who conduct secret bombing raids (67 per cent); politicians who engage in secret wiretapping (71 per cent);

businessmen who make illegal political contributions (81 per cent); and politicians who try to use the Central Intelligence Agency, the Federal Bureau of Investigation and the Secret Service for political purposes or to try to restrict freedom (88 per cent)." "That," Mr. Harris said, "is what has happened in America."[16]

That is statistical confirmation of the obvious: that the former constituency of the corporate-military alliance is in shambles. And it is in this context that the recent inactivity of the left is most disappointing. For if over 80 percent of the American people now find corporate control over the political process dangerous, and an even greater percentage fear politicians who use the secret police, then it means that the American people have regained their senses and that serious concern over real enemies has replaced paranoia about the foreign devil.

This return to sanity occurs at a time when there is much to think about—when basic economic and political questions long dormant are now out there in the public domain where ordinary people can get at them. But without a political framework, the information that has come out is just so much startling data and gossip. It can only become the subject of political debate by being put into the context of coherent issues and programs. America very much needs an active, organized left political force but it must be one that moves away from the style that was useful in the sixties. It is no longer the time to shock but rather to build unity. The experience of foreign revolutions should be presented (when it is accurate to do so) as a source of positive hope and not as a hostile and rude awakening. Nor can the stance of anti-intellectualism be any longer justified at a time when clear and accurate analysis of the American power structure is in great public demand.

Most important of all, the left must abandon the idea that the average American benefits from racism and imperialism. For, as even the labor bureaucrats now recognize, the new era of the multinational corporations disenfranchises the American workers as it does their counterparts in Taiwan, by pitting one against the other. If there are any lingering doubts about the disaffection of the labor vote from Nixon, the following results from a Gallup poll reported at the end of 1972 constitute a statistical denial of the hard-hat image:

> Among labor union members and their families, another new majority target in 1972, Mr. Nixon's approval has dropped from 61 percent to 20 percent in the last year. George Meany, the labor leader, who was neutral in the President's last campaign, is now calling for Mr. Nixon's impeachment.[17]

Unfortunately George Meany is too entrenched in his old ways to chance a real alternative. Such an alternative would have to begin with a program for dismantling the power of Corporate America as it is manifested in all dimensions—advertising, wage determination, output decisions, political contributions. Unless this is done—and it means, in effect, ending the existence of such corporations as centers of power

—the politics of Nixon will continue long after him. Just as the Truman Doctrine was continued by Eisenhower, so too will the Nixon Doctrine be continued by Gerald Ford. For it is not a matter of the personal integrity, individual political outlook of a President, or even the constituency he claims to speak for, but rather of the class interests which he really represents.

In America after Nixon, in the absence of a strong left, power will continue to concentrate in a corporate political structure which is wasteful of our resources, incapable of world-wide planning for economic development, and hence incapable of maintaining peace and prosperity. For the growth and profits of the corporations are not consistent with the long-run needs of a peaceful world. The planning of such units represents an anachronistic restraint on our political imaginations, and their definition of freedom mocks every effort of ordinary human beings to make sense of their world. In a day when increasing numbers of Americans can see this quite easily, the ultra-left politics of alienation of the recent past becomes reactionary. It is encouraging that former Attorney General Ramsay Clark made the issue of the multinationals central to his recent New York Senate campaign. In a formulation quite compatible with those expressed in this book, he charged: "Where is democracy and how can we solve problems if our energy policy is determined by the oil firms, antitrust enforcement by ITT, foreign policy by the multinationals?"[18]

A major problem of the New Left was its frequent

insistence that the college and bohemian community represented the only fruitful base for militant political action. But in the seventies the leadership has more often come from other sectors of the society as in the independent truckers' boycott, consumer revolts, or wildcat strikes. Indeed a recent and in-depth Yankelovich survey concludes:

> Working-class young people in the United States are taking on many of the attitudes on sex, politics, patriotism, religion, the family, morals and life-style that marked college student thinking of five years ago. The result . . . is that workers are becoming increasingly dissatisfied and frustrated at a sense of unfulfillment.[19]

This being the case, we must develop politics which presume that most Americans are capable of progressive thought and identification with the goals of social justice. A significant left force would have to involve the participation of housewives, editors, labor leaders, liberal Senators, as well as the leadership of rank-and-file Americans. Any gap between the left and environmentalists, or youth, or hip, or square, is, in this context, destructive. There is only one basis of unity and that is a denial of the legitimacy of corporate political and economic power. All other differences fall into the category of what Mao has called contradictions among the people. If the thesis of this book is correct as to the role of corporate America then such unity should be a practical possibility, but only if we can overcome the generally corrupting influences, co-option, and divisiveness of the culture within which we must operate.

The thrust of my argument has been a Marxist one—that class struggle is the dominant feature of the current world reality, as it has no doubt been historically. Unless the masses of poorer and ordinary people in the world fundamentally change their relation to the means of production, the outstanding problems of waste, underdevelopment, alienation, and violence will remain and indeed increase.

The timetable of America's New Left was all wrong. America will now go through decades of sustained struggle for change. This is still the richest and most powerful country in the world. Its ruling elite still has many cards to play and victory against it will not come cheaply. As the system weakens it will thrash about more and more dangerously, the citizenry will often be divided by false consciousness, there will be violent hunts for scapegoats, and there is an ever-present danger that as bourgeois life becomes intolerable, racism, religious frenzy, chauvinism, and cultism will temporarily hold sway over sections of the public. As the years of Watergate have demonstrated, there will be frightening, uncertain times, but also hopeful ones in which Americans will come to be more aware. But to be aware without having strong and positive alternatives is to produce a sense of impotence and cynicism.

The New Left of the sixties was weakened by its victories. There have been other models in the world, and indeed in our own history, of people gaining strength from struggle. The example of Vietnam is never too worn for repetition. No people has suffered more and no people has grown so much. The Vietnamese revolution nurtured rather than drained a people, and perception of the social realities made them stronger rather than weaker. This is the lesson that the walking wounded of past causes should learn from the Vietnamese. It is time to clear the decks of guilt and despair, to politely ask the burnt-out cases to take a rest, but to permit others, hopefully many who have never before moved politically, to get on with the work of changing the face of America and its predatory relation to the world. If we look to our own country's history, we will find that the mass of people have snapped back repeatedly from periods of slumber and reaction, from racism and national chauvinism, to wage a higher level of struggle. One of the side effects of the Cold War was to keep this history from us. The history of populism, socialism, and labor struggles has many lessons and is a source of sustenance. It was a tradition of radicalism which once again rose in the mass antiwar and civil rights politics of the sixties, and, now, in the aftermath of the Cold War, faces its best opportunity.

NOTES

Notes to the Preface

1. "Chief Executive Roster: Who Gets the Most Pay," *Forbes*, 15 May 1974, p. 126.

2. Ibid.

3. *San Francisco Examiner*, 27 June 1974.

Notes to Chapter 1

1. Hugh Sidey, "The Response: 'It Gives Me Faith'" (interview with Henry Kissinger), *Time*, 3 September 1973, p. 15.

2. Richard M. Nixon, *U.S. Foreign Policy for the 1970's: Building for Peace. A Report to the Congress*, 25 February 1971, p. 10 (hereafter cited as *Nixon Doctrine*).

3. This seems to me the obvious conclusion to be drawn from a reading of the documents themselves. The reader is referred to U.S. Department of State, *Foreign Relations of the United States: Diplomatic Papers: The Conferences at Malta and Yalta, 1945* (Washington, D.C.: U.S. Government Printing Office, 1955). An example of this "fair exchange" would be the much-publicized Polish election issue. It is clear from the Stalin-Roosevelt dialogues that "free" elections in the final public declaration were a concession to Roosevelt's domestic political needs. Stalin was assured by Roosevelt that election or not he would always have a neighboring government amenable to Soviet interests. In a similar vein, Stalin conceded Greece's place in the Western camp. One particularly blunt summary of this "understanding" is provided in Churchill's memoirs. See Winston S. Churchill, *The Second World War* (Boston: Houghton Mifflin, 1948–1953), VI, pp. 227–228. As Churchill tells it:

> The moment was apt for business, so I said, "Let us settle about our affairs in the Balkans. Your armies are in Rumania and Bulgaria. We have interests, missions, and agents there. Don't let us get at cross-purposes in small ways. So far as Britain and Russia are concerned, how would it do for you to have ninety per cent predominance in Rumania, for us to have ninety per cent of the say in Greece, and go fifty-fifty about Yugoslavia?" While this was being translated I wrote out on a half-sheet of paper:
>
> Rumania
> Russia   90%
> The others   10%

Greece
Great Britain   90%
   (in accord with U.S.A.)
Russia   10%

Yugoslavia   50–50%
Hungary   50–50%

Bulgaria
Russia   75%
The others   25%

I pushed this across to Stalin, who had by then heard the
translation. There was a slight pause. Then he took his
blue pencil and made a large tick upon it, and passed it
back to us. It was all settled in no more time than it
takes to set down. . . .

After this there was a long silence. The pencilled paper
lay in the centre of the table. At length I said, "Might it
not be thought rather cynical if it seemed we had disposed
of these issues, so fateful to millions of people, in such an
offhand manner? Let us burn the paper." "No, you keep
it," said Stalin.

Even so staunch a liberal as Arthur Schlesinger, Jr. was once instrumental in selling the "Soviet betrayal theory" to the American
public. See his *Vital Center* (Boston: Houghton Mifflin Company,
1949), pp. 92–96. Schlesinger reversed himself twenty years later. He
now admits that Stalin's "initial objectives were very probably not
world conquest but Russian security." See "Origins of the Cold
War," *Foreign Affairs* 46, no. 1 (October 1967): 36. For further
documentation see Diane Shaver Clemens, *Yalta* (New York: Oxford
University Press, 1970), pp. 268–270.

4. But Browder's plan to dissolve the American Communist Party
and transform it into an educational society went too far afield
from Stalin's postwar strategy of cooperation. Even the famous
Duclos Letter by the French Communist leader, while attacking
him, reaffirmed the "necessity" to support the spirit of both Tehran
and Yalta with a broad front of antifascist forces. See Jacques
Duclos, "A propos de la dissolution du Parti Communiste Améri-
cain," *Cahiers du Communisme,* Numéro 6 (Paris: April 1945), p. 21.

5. Strobe Talbott, ed., *Khrushchev Remembers: The Last Testa-
ment* (Boston: Little, Brown and Company, 1974), p. 355.

6. *Nixon Doctrine,* p. 5.

7. Ibid.

8. Ibid., pp. 10–17.

9. Ibid., p. 13.

Notes to Chapter 2

1. Henry A. Kissinger, *The Troubled Partnership* (New York: Mc-Graw-Hill Book Company, 1965), p. 5.

2. Ibid.

3. Ibid., p. 7.

4. Ibid., p. 9.

5. Ibid.

6. Ibid.

7. Ibid., p. 10.

8. Ibid.

9. Henry Brandon, *The Retreat of American Power* (New York: Doubleday & Company, 1973), p. 39.

10. Henry A. Kissinger, "Central Issues of American Foreign Policy," in *Agenda for the Nation,* ed. Kermit Gordon (Washington, D.C.: The Brookings Institute, 1968), p. 613.

11. Richard M. Nixon, *U.S. Foreign Policy for the 1970's: Building for Peace. A Report to the Congress,* 25 February 1971, p. 10 (hereafter cited as *Nixon Doctrine*).

12. Kissinger, "Central Issues of American Foreign Policy," p. 591.

13. Henry A. Kissinger, *American Foreign Policy, Three Essays* (New York: W. W. Norton & Company, 1969), p. 93.

14. Ibid., pp. 91–92.

15. Ibid., p. 92.

16. Ibid.

17. Ibid.

18. Ibid., p. 79.

19. *Nixon Doctrine,* pp. 10–11.

20. Ibid., p. 17.

21. Ibid., pp. 121–122.

Notes to Chapter 3

1. Henry A. Kissinger, *American Foreign Policy, Three Essays* (New York: W. W. Norton & Company, 1969), p. 97.

2. Henry Brandon, *The Retreat of American Power* (New York: Doubleday & Company, 1973), p. 26.

3. Bernard and Marvin Kalb, *Kissinger* (Boston: Little Brown and Company, 1974), p. 16.

4. Ibid., p. 56.

5. Ibid.

6. Nelson Rockefeller, *The Rockefeller Report on the Americas* (Chicago: Quadrangle Books, 1969), p. 8.

7. *New York Post,* 7 April 1969.

8. Rockefeller, *Rockefeller Report,* p. 60.

9. Ibid.

10. *New York Times,* 30 September 1973, p. 61.

11. A. James Reichley, "Let's Reform Campaign Financing—But Let's Do It Right," *Fortune,* December 1973, p. 97.

12. Ibid., p. 95.

13. Ibid.

14. Ibid., p. 96.

15. North American Congress on Latin America, *Latin America and Empire Report* 7, no. 9 (November 1973): 8 (hereafter cited as *NACLA Report*).

16. Sanford Rose, "The Push to Make Them Pay More Taxes," *Fortune,* August 1973, p. 57.

17. *NACLA Report,* pp. 13–14.

18. *Los Angeles Times,* 30 September 1973.

19. *Los Angeles Times,* 29 September 1973.

20. *Washington Post,* 7 August 1973.

21. *New York Times,* 19 August 1974, p. 1.

22. Ibid., p. 38.

23. Ibid.

24. *San Francisco Chronicle,* 7 February 1974, p. 10.

25. Ibid.

Notes to Chapter 4

1. Paul A. Baran and Paul M. Sweezy, *Monopoly Capital* (New York: Monthly Review Press, 1966), p. vii.

2. Gardiner C. Means, "Foreword," in John M. Blair, *Economic Concentration: Structure, Behavior and Public Policy* (New York: Harcourt Brace Jovanovich, Inc., 1972), p. vi.

3. Paul A. Samuelson, *Economics,* 9th Edition (New York: McGraw-Hill Book Company, 1973), p. 48.

4. Ibid.

5. Ibid., p. ix.

6. Ibid., p. 849.

7. Karl Marx, *Capital,* ed. Frederick Engels, trans. from the 3rd German edition by Samuel Moore and Edward Aveling (New York: International Publishers, 1967), p. 626.

8. Ibid., pp. 762–763.

9. Samuelson, *Economics,* p. 862.

10. V. I. Lenin, *Imperialism, The Highest Stage of Capitalism,* (Peking: Foreign Languages Press, 1970), p. 43.

11. Ibid., p. 106.

Notes to Chapter 5

1. Sanford Rose, "Multinational Corporations in a Tough New World," *Fortune,* August 1973, p. 134.

2. Sanford Rose, "The Push to Make Them Pay More Taxes," *Fortune,* August 1973, p. 57.

3. United Nations, *Multinational Corporations in World Development,* a publication of the Department of Economic and Social Affairs (ST/ECA/190), 1973, p. 7 (hereafter cited as *UN Mutinational Study*).

4. *Fortune* interview with Robert B. Stobaugh and Sidney M. Robbins, "How the Multinationals Play the Money Game," *Fortune,* August 1973, p. 61.

5. Ibid.

6. Harry Magdoff, "The Logic of Imperialism," *Social Policy,* September/October 1970, pp. 13–15.

7. *UN Multinational Study,* p. 187.

8. Ibid., p. 193.

9. William P. Rogers, *United States Foreign Policy 1972, A Report of the Secretary of State* (Department of State publication no. 8699, General Foreign Policy Series 274, April 1973), p. 11.

10. Ibid., p. 15.

11. Ibid.

12. Rose, "The Push to Make Them Pay More Taxes," p. 57.

13. Ibid., p. 54.

14. Ibid., p. 55.

15. Ibid.

16. Rogers, *United States Foreign Policy 1972,* p. 13.

17. *UN Multinational Study,* p. 13.

18. Ibid., pp. 13–14.

19. Ibid., p. 16.

20. Ibid.

21. Ibid., p. 15.

22. Ibid., p. 16.

23. Ibid., p. 17.

24. Ibid.

25. Ibid., p. 18.

26. Ibid., p. 20.

27. Ibid.

28. Osvaldo Sunkel, "Big Business and *'Dependencia,'*" *Foreign Affairs* 50, no. 3 (April 1972): 527–528.

29. Ibid., p. 519.

Notes to Chapter 6

1. Douglas Dowd, *The Twisted Dream* (Cambridge, Mass.: Winthrop Publishers, 1974), p. 70.

2. "U.S. Multinationals—The Dimming of America," a report prepared for the AFL-CIO Maritime Trades Department Executive Board Meeting, 15–16 February 1973, in the *Hearings before the Subcommittee on International Trade of the Committee on Finance,* U.S. Senate, 93rd Congress, 1st Session, February 26, 27, 28, and March 1 and 6, 1973; p. 488 (hereafter cited as *Long Hearings*).

3. Arvind V. Phatak, *Evolution of World Enterprises* (New York: American Management Association, 1971), pp. 40–41.

4. Ibid., p. 41.

5. Ibid., p. 40.

6. *San Francisco Chronicle,* 7 January 1974.

7. "Disclosure of Corporate Ownership," a report prepared by the U.S. Senate Subcommittees on Intergovernmental Relations, and Budgeting, Management, and Expenditures of the Committee on Government Operations (Metcalf and Muskie Hearings), 27 December 1973, p. 5.

8. Ibid.

9. Ibid., p. 8.

10. John M. Blair, *Economic Concentration: Structure, Behavior and Public Policy* (New York: Harcourt Brace Jovanovich, Inc., 1972), p. 475.

11. Ibid.

12. Ibid., p. 482.

13. Ibid., p. 486.

14. United Nations, *Multinational Corporations in World Development*, a publication of the Department of Economic and Social Affairs (ST/ECA/190), 1973, pp. 130–131.

15. Ibid.

16. "Union Carbide's International Investment Benefits the U.S. Economy," in *Multinational Corporations*, a compendium of papers submitted to the U.S. Senate Subcommittee on International Trade of the Committee on Finance, 21 February 1973, pp. 457–458.

17. Phatak, *Evolution of World Enterprises*, p. 44.

18. Ibid., p. 43.

19. *Long Hearings*, p. 106.

20. Ibid., pp. 380–381.

21. Ibid., p. 73.

22. Gene E. Bradley and Edward C. Bursk, "Multinationalism and the 29th Day," *Harvard Business Review*, January–February 1972, p. 45.

23. *Long Hearings*, p. 77.

24. Ibid., p. 451.

25. Ibid., p. 106.

26. Ibid., p. 451.

Notes to Chapter 7

1. *New York Times*, 17 April 1973, p. 26.

2. Joe Stork, "Middle East Oil and the Energy Crisis: Part One," *MERIP Reports*, no. 20 (September 1973): 3.

3. E. B. Weiss, "The Third World Starts Emerging as a Big Consumer Market," *Advertising Age*, 10 December 1973, p. 47.

4. Edmund Faltermayer, "Metals: The Warning Signals Are Up," *Fortune*, October 1972, p. 109.

5. Stork, "Middle East Oil: Part One," p. 3.

6. Edmund Faltermayer, "The Energy 'Joyride' Is Over," *Fortune*, September 1972, p. 99.

7. David Wise and Thomas B. Ross, *The Invisible Government* (New York: Random House, 1964), pp. 110–113; Victor Marchetti and John D. Marks, *The CIA and the Cult of Intelligence* (New York: Alfred A. Knopf, 1974), p. 29.

8. Stork, "Middle East Oil: Part One," p. 14.

9. Ibid., p. 19.

10. Ibid.

11. Ibid., p. 14.

12. Ibid., p. 16.

13. Joe Stork, "Middle East Oil and the Energy Crisis: Part Two," MERIP Reports, no. 21 (October 1973): 7–8.

14. Ibid., p. 9.

15. *New York Times*, 3 June 1974, p. 1.

16. James E. Akins, "The Oil Crisis: This Time the Wolf is Here," *Foreign Affairs* 51, no. 3 (April 1973): 473–476.

17. Ibid., p. 475.

18. Ibid., p. 484.

19. Ibid., p. 485.

20. Ibid., p. 488.

21. Ibid., p. 474.

22. Ibid.

23. Stork, "Middle East Oil: Part Two," p. 21.

24. Akins, "The Oil Crisis," p. 489.

25. *San Francisco Chronicle*, 26 January 1974.

26. Stork, "Middle East Oil: Part Two," p. 22.

27. Robert S. McNamara, *One Hundred Countries, Two Billion People* (New York: Praeger Publishers, 1973), p. 75.

28. Ibid.

29. Ibid.

30. Ibid., p. 73.

31. *New York Times*, Section 3, *Business and Finance*, 13 January 1974, p. 1.

32. Ibid.

33. Ibid.

Notes to Chapter 8

1. William P. Rogers, *United States Foreign Policy 1972, A Report of the Secretary of State* (Department of State publication no. 8699, General Foreign Policy Series 274, April 1973), pp. 41–42.

2. Ibid., p. 42.

3. Ibid., p. 43.

4. Ibid., pp. 44–45.

5. "Multinationals: Heros? Or Villains?," *Forbes*, 15 May 1973, p. 266.

6. *United Nations Statistical Yearbook, 1972* (New York: United Nations, 1973), p. 12.

7. Ibid., pp. 628–629.

8. Ibid., pp. 539–540.

9. Ibid., pp. 506–507.

10. Ibid., pp. 760–767.

11. Harry Magdoff, *The Age of Imperialism* (New York: Monthly Review Press, 1969), p. 54.

12. Pierre Jalée, *The Third World in World Economy* (New York: Monthly Review Press, 1969), pp. 37–38.

13. Edmund Faltermayer, "Metals: The Warning Signals Are Up," *Fortune*, October 1972, p. 109.

14. Ibid.

Notes to Chapter 9

1. Robert S. McNamara, *One Hundred Countries, Two Billion People* (New York: Praeger Publishers, 1973), p. 54.

2. Ibid., p. 74.

3. Ibid., p. 77.

4. Ibid., p. 30.

5. Ibid., p. 90.

6. Ibid., p. 88.

7. Ibid.

8. "International Advertising," *Advertising Age*, 21 November 1973, p. 184.

9. Ibid., p. 20.

10. Raymond Vernon, *The Economic and Political Consequences of Multinational Enterprise: An Anthology* (Boston: Harvard University Division of Research/Graduate School of Business Administration, 1972), p. 64.

11. Ibid., p. 66.

12. Ibid., p. 67.

13. Ibid.

14. Ibid., p. 68.

15. Ibid., p. 69.

16. Ibid., pp. 69–70.

Notes to Chapter 10

1. *Wall Street Journal*, 20 September 1973, p. 36.

2. *New York Times*, 17 August 1974, p. 2.

3. *Wall Street Journal*, 20 September 1973, p. 36.

4. Ibid.

5. E. B. Weiss, "The Third World Starts Emerging as a Big Consumer Market," *Advertising Age*, 10 December 1973, p. 45.

6. Ibid., p. 47.

7. Ibid.

8. *New York Times,* 8 October 1973, p. 2

9. Weiss, "The Third World Starts Emerging," p. 47.

10. Ibid.

11. Ibid.

12. Robert S. McNamara, *One Hundred Countries, Two Billion People* (New York: Praeger Publishers, 1973), p. 102.

13. Ibid., p. 103.

14. Ibid.

15. Ibid., p. 107.

16. Ibid., p. 106.

17. Ibid., p. 16.

18. Weiss, "The Third World Starts Emerging," p. 47.

Notes to Chapter 11

1. "Kahn Eyes Bright Prospect for Korea," *Korean Newsreview* 2, no. 47 (24 November 1973): 12–13.

2. Richard M. Nixon, *U.S. Foreign Policy for the 1970's: Building for Peace. A Report to the Congress,* 25 February 1971, p. 96.

3. Tony Patrick, "Park Tenses for the Challenge," *Far Eastern Economic Review,* 7 January 1974, p. 36.

4. *The Morgan Guaranty Survey* (published monthly by Morgan Guaranty Trust Company of New York), October 1970, p. 8.

5. Ibid.

6. *New York Times,* 28 May 1974, p. 38.

7. Patrick, "Park Tenses," p. 36.

8. *Journal of Commerce* (Canada), 29 October 1973, p. 6S.

9. B. F. Wideman, "Korean Chauvinism," *Far Eastern Economic Review,* 5 March 1973, p. 39.

10. Ibid.

11. Ibid.

12. Patrick, "Park Tenses," p. 36.

13. *New York Times,* Section 4, *The Week in Review,* 30 August 1970, p. 1.

14. Ibid.

15. "Korea: Japan Moves in on U.S. Business," *Business Week,* 1 September 1973, p. 50.

16. Joseph Z. Reday, "Far East Business," *The Oriental Economist,* October 1971, p. 36.

17. Patrick, "Park Tenses," p. 38.

18. Ibid., p. 39.

19. "A New Storm Hits the World Bank," *Business Week,* 26 September 1970, p. 100.

20. Patrick, "Park Tenses," p. 39.

21. Ibid.

22. "Korea: Japan Moves in," p. 50.

23. "Korean Work Law Revisions Ensure Peace, Shackle Labor," *Business Asia,* 6 April 1973, p. 106.

24. Patrick, "Park Tenses," p. 36.

25. Ellen Brun, "North Korea: A Case of Real Development," *Monthly Review,* June 1970, p. 28.

26. "Rice Shortage Worries Korea," *Asian Industry,* March 1971, p. 71.

27. "ROK Economy Again on Swelling Tide," *The Oriental Economist,* July 1973, p. 16.

28. *New York Times,* 17 August 1974, p. 2.

29. *United Nations Statistical Yearbook, 1972* (New York: United Nations, 1973), p. 749.

30. "Labor Law and Practice in the Republic of Korea" (U.S. G.P.O.: Bureau of Labor Statistics Report no. 361, 1969), pp. 7–8.

31. *Washington Post,* 18 December 1970.

32. Ibid.

33. Ibid.

34. Ibid.

35. Ibid.

36. Ibid.

37. "Korea: Land on the Move," *New York Times* supplement, 4 November 1973, p. 11.

38. Ibid.

39. Ibid.

40. "General Motors' South Korean Move Underlines Asia-Pacific Growth Prospects," *Business Asia,* 21 April 1972, p. 121.

Notes to Chapter 12

1. Orville Schell, "In China All Waste is Treasure," *Clear Creek,* February 1972, pp. 24–28 (This article is based on a longer, unpublished version.).

2. Ibid.

3. "Kirin's Chemical Industry Makes Some Changes," *China Reconstructs,* August 1972, pp. 20–21.

4. Ibid., pp. 21–22.

5. Chi Wei, "Turning the Harmful Into the Beneficial," *Peking Review,* 28 January 1972, p. 5.

6. Ibid.

7. Shen Wen, "Going in for Farming in an Industrial City," *Peking Review,* 5 March 1971, p. 10.

8. Ibid., p. 8.

9. "Shanghai Uses Waste Water to Irrigate Farmland," *Peking Review,* 19 March 1971, p. 27.

10. Chi, "Harmful Into Beneficial," p. 7.

11. Daily press release, English edition, 25 August 1973, Peking, New China News Agency.

12. Schell, "In China," (unpublished version), p. 8.

13. Ibid.

14. Tang Ke, "China's Stand on the Question of Human Environment," (transcript of a speech by the Vice-Minister of Fuel and Chemical Industries, leader of the Chinese delegation to the First United Nations Conference on the Human Environment, 5–16 June 1972 in Stockholm, Sweden), *Peking Review*, 16 June 1972, p. 8.

15. Ibid.

16. Ibid.

17. Paul R. Ehrlich, *The Population Bomb* (New York: Ballantine Books, 1968), p. 165.

18. Ibid., p. 166.

19. Ibid., p. 160.

20. Ibid., pp. 161–162.

21. Ibid., pp. 162–163.

22. Tang, "China's Stand," p. 8.

23. Ibid.

24. James Keddie, "The Mass Unemployment Explosion," *Far Eastern Economic Review*, 31 December 1973, p. 41.

25. Ibid.

26. Ibid.

27. Ibid., p. 43.

28. Tang, "China's Stand," p. 5.

29. Ibid., p. 6.

30. *Economic Reporter*, July–September 1973, p. 16.

31. "Chinese Observer on Population Question," (This is a slightly abridged version of a speech by the Chinese observer Yu Wang at the Seventeenth Session of the United Nations Population Commission, held on 2 November 1973.), *Peking Review*, 7 December 1973, pp. 10–11.

Notes to Chapter 13

1. Houari Boumediene, from an unofficial translation of Boume-
diene's speech to the United Nations Sixth Special Session on Raw
Materials, held in April 1974, released to the press by the Algerian
Consulate, 10 April 1974, pp. 3–4.

2. Ibid., p. 52.

3. Teng Hsiao-ping, "Chairman of Chinese Delegation Teng Hsiao-
ping's Speech," *Peking Review,* 19 April 1974, p. 6.

4. Ibid.

5. Ibid., p. 7.

6. Boumediene, Speech to the UN Special Session, p. 25.

7. Teng, "Chinese Delegation Speech," p. 11.

8. United Nations Press Release, GA/4963, 11 April 1974, p. 9.

9. Boumediene, Speech to the UN Special Session, p. 25.

10. Ibid., p. 9.

11. Ibid., p. 12.

12. Ibid., p. 13.

13. Ibid., p. 18.

14. United Nations Center for Economic and Social Information,
Note/247, 9 April 1974, p. 1; "Evolution of Basic Commodity Prices
Since 1950," UN Document A/9544, 2 April 1974, p. 3.

15. United Nations Press Release, GA/4970, 15 April 1974, p. 3.

16. Ibid.

17. Ibid., p. 6.

18. *New York Times,* 3 April 1974, p. 13.

19. *New York Times,* 16 April 1974, p. 12.

20. *New York Times,* 3 April 1974, p. 13.

21. "Where George Shultz Fits in at Bechtel," *Business Week,* 18
May 1974, p. 76.

22. Ibid., p. 76 and "Construction's Man of the Year: Stephen D. Bechtel, Jr.," *Engineering News-Record*, 21 February 1974, p. 31.

23. "Where George Shultz Fits in," p. 76.

24. Boumediene, Speech to the UN Special Session, p. 42.

25. United Nations Press Release, GA/4970, 15 April 1974, p. 4.

26. *Report of the Secretary of Defense, James R. Schlesinger, to the Congress on the Fiscal Year 1975 Defense Budget and Fiscal Years 1975–1979 Defense Program* (U.S. G.P.O., 4 March 1974), p. 2.

27. Ibid., p. 35.

28. *Washington Post*, 31 May 1974.

Notes to Chapter 14

1. *Washington Post*, 1 June 1974.

2. Ibid.

3. Ibid.

4. "An American Trade Union View of International Trade and Investment," paper submitted by AFL-CIO in *Multinational Corporations,* a compendium of papers submitted to the U.S. Senate Subcommittee on International Trade of the Committee on Finance, 21 February 1973, p. 69 (hereafter cited as *Multinational Corporations*).

5. Ibid., p. 70.

6. Ibid., p. 72.

7. Ibid.

8. Hugh Sidey, "The Response: 'It Gives Me Faith'" (interview with Henry Kissinger), *Time*, 3 September 1973, p. 15.

9. Walter J. Hickel, *Who Owns America?* (New York: Paperback Library, 1971), p. 9.

10. Ibid., p. 295.

11. *Multinational Corporations*, p. 71.

12. Sidey, "The Response," p. 15.

13. Stephen Hymer and Robert Rowthorn, "Multinational Corporations and International Oligopoly: The Non-American Challenge," in *The International Corporation*, ed. Charles P. Kindleberger (Cambridge, Mass.: M.I.T. Press, 1970), p. 88.

14. Henry Brandon, *The Retreat of American Power* (New York: Doubleday & Company, 1973), p. 350.

15. *New York Times*, 21 January 1974, p. 16.

16. Ibid.

17. Ibid.

18. *New York Times*, Section 4, *The Week in Review*, 18 August 1974, p. 7.

19. *New York Times*, 22 May 1974, p. 45.

ACKNOWLEDGMENTS

After happily signing my contract with McGraw-Hill I went off on a three-month trip to North Vietnam, China, and Korea only to learn that I had become a sedentary, self-indulgent, and bourgeois oaf.

Fortunately I returned to a Berkeley that was far less restrained than the media would have it and during the writing of this book have been supported, attacked, criticized, and loved by a group of friends and students, many of whom are half my age. I don't know what goes on in the courses of the paid faculty at UC Berkeley, but this book emerged out of three years of encounters with a dedicated and unintimidated group in our illegitimate Thursday night class. They challenged my cynicism and other cholesterols of the spirit. In particular, I want to mention Rachel Blau, Joe Doyle, Mike Chinn, James Farnum, Leoni Fisher, Glen Janken, Rick Jurgens, Bob Korda, Steve Liebman, Allan Miller, Patty Miller, Mia Monroe, Betty Ryan, Gail Wender, and Stu Wasserman.

Steve Wasserman played a decisive role as researcher, editor, king of the footnotes, political foil, and constant energizer. He should go on to write better books than this one. Ann Dowie did the original editing, heroically untwisted my P.S. 89 grammar and persistently flagged down my rhetoric.

I live in a house with seven people who had to put up with my writer's block, that excuse for bad tempers and broken windows. The book was very much influenced by daily political debate with Anne Weills, Daniel and Jonathan Siegel, and Marcia Meyers. My son Christopher kept reminding me that anyone over five can write a book of some kind and that sometimes it's more important to wrestle and go fishing. During the writing of this book we criss-crossed the country on Amtrak, and often his first-grader's openness made him an invaluable guide, translator, and friend.

There are also some political veterans who have stayed young and hopeful, and who read the manuscript after I gave them a lot of my good wine. Susan Adelman, Stu Bishop, Mark Bramhall, Dick Fine, John and Nancy Frappier, Terry Karl, Larry Mann, Linda Morse, Tony Platt, Stanley Scheinbaum, Orville Schell, and Lenny Weinglass all pushed me in good directions. I owe Frank Bardecke, Lawrence Ferlinghetti, Dugald Stermer, Frank Gonzales, and Christopher Weills for much help in the past.

I traveled in Asia with Andrew Truskier and Jan Austin, both of whom provided a model for me of commitment and humanism. They worked with the

Asia Information Group (now Internews), which along with NACLA (North American Congress on Latin America), URPE (Union of Radical Political Economists), the Pacific Studies Center, and MERIP (Middle East Research and Information Project) furnished much of the documentation. While these groups are not responsible for the ideas in this book I do want to express my respect for their work.

In the big bad city I had people like Joyce Johnson and Cyrilly Abels to provide reassurance that a book is not after all a product, and that the writer too has to be happy with the changes. The most eclectic group of writers has come to rely on Cyrilly's integrity and good taste. Joyce is the best editor in the world and a good friend. Her assistant, Veronica Windholz, was always helpful and effective.

If there is an Eastern Intellectual Establishment it does not include Stanley Aronowitz, Richard Barnet, Susan Crille, Judy Collins, Eugene, Sheila, and Bitsy Lyne, Richard Levine, Marcus and Barbara Raskin, David Rieff, Susan Sontag, Milton and Judith Viorst, or Margaret Wolf. I am grateful for their fanatical devotion to Szechuan cooking.

Susan Markham Lyne provided critical guidance at every stage in the writing and production. She designed the cover, ruthlessly exposed sloppy thinking, rewrote, edited, and fortunately has never learned to type. With humor and diligence, Susan consistently combated my liberalism, and along with Joyce Johnson and Steve Wasserman, made the manuscript into a book.

ABOUT THE AUTHOR

Born in the Bronx in 1936, Robert Scheer attended New York City public schools. After graduation from the City College of New York in 1958, he continued his studies at Syracuse University as Maxwell Fellow in Economics and Public Administration and at the University of California at Berkeley as a Fellow at the Center for Chinese Studies. He later taught Economics and Politics at both City College and Berkeley and for the last three years at the San Francisco campus of Antioch College.

Over the past fifteen years, he has traveled extensively to North and South Vietnam, North Korea, the Middle East, North Africa, Cuba, and China—where he was one of the first Western visitors after the Cultural Revolution.

Mr. Scheer was with *Ramparts* from 1964 to 1969 as managing editor, and in 1969 was editor-in-chief. He is the author of *How the U.S. Got Involved in*

Vietnam and *Cuba: Tragedy in Our Hemisphere* (with Maurice Zeitlin). He also edited the *Diaries of Che Guevara* and Eldridge Cleaver's *Post-Prison Writings and Speeches.*